Secrets to Date By

Secrets to Date By

JULA JANE

JULA

PUBLISHING

For information, contact
JULA Publishing
700 Park Regency Place, Suite 1402
Atlanta, Georgia 30326.

JULA Publishing books may be purchased for
educational, business, or promotional use.
For information, please write:
Special Markets Department,
JULA Publishing,
700 Park Regency Place, Suite 1402
Atlanta, Georgia 30326.

Cover illustration: Jason Brooks, *www.brooks.design@virgin.net*
Editor: Karen Brailsford, *brailsten@aim.com*

Library of Congress Cataloging-in-Publication Data
Jane, Jula
Secrets to Date By / Jula Jane
ISBN—13: 978–0–9799715–0–1
ISBN—10: 0–9799715–0–0   2007910221

Visit: *www.jula-publishing.com* and *www.julajane.com*
for more information.

*In loving memory of
my great-grandmother, Jula Jane*

Contents

Acknowledgments

A wealth of gratitude goes out to so many for their contributions to and patience for this well-meaning perfectionist:

Keith Coggins, for believing in me even when I didn't believe in myself. You have given me so many gifts—my vision, my smile, and most recently, my dream come true. Thank you, baby—for everything you do and everything you are.

Donna McKinnie, for being a sounding board for all of my crazy ideas, and simply for always being there. Your friendship means the world to me.

Mom, for instilling the belief that anything is possible. I think I can, I think I can.

A special thank you to my sister for setting the bar so high. You make me want to be a better person, and I love you for it.

To my brother, for helping me understand that men are born this way.

Dad, for giving me your entrepreneurial genes. You saved my life.

G.W.T.S.P and granddaddy, for taking care of little Nikki when I needed time to think and write, and for always being my biggest fans.

Nikki Jane, for being a woman's best friend and a loyal companion.

Gina Bishop, for sharing your book-worthy dating stories, and for your friendship.

Danielle DeHass, for being my wing woman when I was single, and for always making me laugh.

My editor, Karen Brailsford, for dotting my i's and crossing my t's. You are truly talented and a pleasure to work with.

Jason Brooks, for being the illustrator who could. Your work is amazing and your professionalism, appreciated.

Gerry Stoner, for your knowledgeable advice and useful tips and, of course, your typesetting abilities.

Artefacto, for giving me a launching pad—and a beautiful one at that.

TwoVital, for capturing the real me.

George Foster, for doing the best with what you had to work with. It was a pleasure working with you.

Toren Anderson, for seeing the big picture and running with it. You have a good eye and a great gift.

Bethany Brown, for letting me stand over your shoulder. It made all the difference in the world.

To all the people who lent a helping hand, a suggestion or a thought, their guidance and criticism—and a shoulder to cry on when I needed it most. I can't thank you enough.

A heartfelt thank you to Miles Neiman for giving an unknown columnist her big break. I'll be eternally grateful.

And most of all, to all the men and women who write to me and share their most intimate stories. You made this book possible.

Thank you.

Introduction

The date was September 21, 1979. I was five years old and full of curiosity about life and where we come from, why we're here, why the grass is green and the sky blue—but most of all, I was curious about boys.

Ah yes, the other sex. How odd and magnificent they seemed to me—one minute they were pulling my hair and the next, they were passing half of their sandwiches to me. Strange, indeed.

That morning, I lay as snug as a bug in my toasty warm bed, and as the sun began to rise and the birds and the bees began to sing, a smile came across my face. I began to giggle uncontrollably. I had waited for this day all my life, envying my older sister for her maturity and independence. At long last, it was finally here—my entrance into the social scene, otherwise known as Kindergarten.

Lost in my vivid imagination, I couldn't hear my mother calling for me to come to breakfast, that is until the smell of bacon wafted through my bedroom door and danced around my nose, begging me to get out of bed. I couldn't resist and made my way into the kitchen. There stood my precious mother welcoming me, her arms out-stretched. She scooped me up and began her remarkable pep talk.

"Jula Bula Bug (her pet name for me), today is your first day of school and I just know you're going to love it. You're going to meet lots of wonderful boys and girls, and have so much fun. When you get to the classroom door, I want you to put on a strong face, walk in with your head held high, and learn as much as you can."

And so I did . . .

I'll never forget that day as long as I live. That was the day that launched my fascination with male-female dynamics—"the dance," as I like to call it. It quickly became quite clear to me that boys and girls are different from each other in so many ways, and that we have a hard time communicating. But *why*, I wondered.

Twenty-eight years have passed and since then, I've gathered days upon days of research, and years upon years of studies—both through personal experience, and from thousands of interviews, conversations, books, movies and magazines. You name it, I studied it. I have organized all of this invaluable information quite nicely and neatly in my mobile filing cabinet, otherwise known as my mind—with additional copies attached closely to my heart. One could say I have a Ph.D. in relationship reality.

A few years ago, I decided to put that knowledge to good use and began writing a relationship advice column called "Dear Jula." The column answers the most pressing questions about the opposite sex. I hear from both men and women, which gives me a balanced perspective on dating and relationships. I absolutely love what I do because I feel I make a difference in people's lives, especially after they write back telling me how my advice has helped them.

Because my column is doing so well and has been helping so many people, I thought it important to base a book on my findings and experiences—and here it is. Written from the heart, *Secrets to Date By* is designed to inspire you to become the best that you can possibly be, to teach you how to date successfully—and to motivate you to change your life for the better. Look at me as your coach, a well-trained, highly-motivated, results-oriented coach. This book is my training manual for you.

I've included relevant questions and answers from my column, as well as worksheets, quizzes, and, of course, juicy secrets. You can flip through until you find something that relates to you, or read your manual front to back. It's up to you.

My mission is for you to go out on a succession of amazing dates; to fall in love and enjoy great sex; and to never have to wait by the phone again. But most of all, I want you to have fun. If you read your manual, do the exercises and make the decision to have a happy, healthy dating life, you will absolutely succeed.

So let's get started.

Secrets to Date By

Chapter 1

It's Raining Men

**Secret #1: A Great Man Isn't Hard to Find . . .
You've Just Got to Know Where to Look**

There are fish in the sea better than have ever been caught.
—Irish saying

Hallelujah! It's raining men! Do you remember this Weather Girls song? Sing it again and again. *Hallelujah! It's raining men!* Ladies, this is your new theme song. I want you to hum it, sing it and belt it out until you believe it. And once you believe it, I want you to *feel* it. And once you feel it, I want you to *live* it.

Whoever said, "There are no good men left," was wrong. In fact, the odds are in your favor: 44 percent of adult Americans are single, which means there are over 100 million unattached men and women just wandering around looking for love. There are literally millions of great guys waiting to be discovered. It's just that Ms. Naysayer (No good men, left? Humph!) wasn't looking in all the right places.

So where does a single woman meet a man? That's the burning question on everyone's lips. The answer is (drum roll, please . . .) OUTSIDE! That's right—*outside*. Confused? Disappointed? Don't be. I'll lay it out for you: He's outside. That means he's not in your apartment, hiding behind the sofa, and he's not under your bed, playing hide-and-go seek. He's outside in the real world living his life and hoping to one day meet the woman of his dreams—you!

HOTSPOTS FOR MEETING HUNKS

- Restaurant Bar
- Hotel Lounge
- Sporting Events
- Church Singles Group
- Grocery Store
- Gym
- Gallery Openings
- Cocktail Parties
- Gas Station
- Home Depot / Lowes
- Electronics Store
- Charity Events
- Wine Tastings
- Pool Hall / Pub
- Bookstore
- Coffee House
- Bar / Nightclub
- Las Vegas Casinos
- Work Functions
- Networking Parties
- Speed Dating Events
- Volunteer
- Craig's List
- The Park
- The Mall
- BYOB (Bring Your Old Boyfriend) Parties
- Same Places / New Cities

That means you have to leave the confines of your home and venture out, if you want to meet a man. If this sounds too scary for you, take a breath and relax; I'm going to hold your hand and teach you the do's and don'ts of dating. By the time you've finished reading this book, you'll be so ready to get out there and date that *nothing* will be able to stop you—not even *you!*

What do I mean by "not even you?" As odd as this sounds, the truth is, sometimes you stand in your own way. You hold yourself back from going after what you want, even when you know you should be taking action. If this sounds familiar and you are in search of a cure, I can help. The first step is to recognize the root of the problem. I have a four-letter word for your disease: F-E-A-R. Fear. You fear the unknown, you fear failure, and you fear rejection. Your fear is what keeps you from living your life to the fullest.

This fear factor resides in most women and is nothing to be ashamed of. You will overcome it. Maybe not in a day, and maybe not by the end of this book, but maybe, just maybe, you'll be free of your fear by the end of say, next week. That sounds reasonable, doesn't it?

NOT JUST ANY WOMAN

That's right! You're not just any woman. No sir, you're a *great* woman and don't you ever forget it. You deserve to be loved, honored, and cherished by friends, family, coworkers, and most of all, by a *Great Man*.

Do you know what it is about you that makes you so great? Do you know why you deserve to be loved, honored and cherished? I didn't think so. So here's what I suggest: I want you to do the following brief exercise. By the end of it, I guarantee that you'll know.

Read the example below and then follow my instructions. Go ahead. Don't be afraid. I'm right here.

GREAT WOMAN WORKSHEET (EXAMPLE)

What's special about me?	I have gorgeous thick red hair and dazzling green eyes. I laugh out loud, cry during romantic movies and sing in the shower. I have a dimple in my left cheek and a slightly-crooked nose. I'm a bit neurotic and extremely organized. I dance around the house, hoping no one sees me. But if they do, I put on a show—I'm a bit of a ham. I love people and I love life.
How do I treat other people?	I'm kind to animals, treat my friends like gold and cherish my family. I treat a Great Man like a king. I

	put him first in my life, show him nothing but respect, and I love him the way I want to be loved: unconditionally.
What do I do to better myself?	I exercise as often as my schedule permits, I try to learn a new word every day, and I read fashion magazines to keep up with the latest trends.
What are my fears?	I fear breaking a nail, not because I'm girly, but because it hurts. I fear one of my extensions will come out during sex. I fear public speaking. I fear losing a loved one. I fear facing my fears.
What are my dreams?	One day I hope to make a difference in someone's life. Not in a "I let someone in front of me in line" kind of difference, but in a "I saved someone's life" kind of difference. I want to write a book and see it on the shelf at Barnes & Noble *and* Borders. I'm dreaming, so I may as well dream big.

Now it's time for you to put pen to paper and write down the answers to these very same thought-provoking questions: 1) What's special about me? 2) How do I treat other people? 3) What do I do to better myself? 4) What are my fears? 5) What are my dreams?

Don't compare yourself to other people, just focus on you. This exercise may make you feel a little uncomfortable at first. Just relax. It's meant to remind you of just how unique you truly are.

THERE'S A METHOD TO MY MADNESS

How's the ego feeling right about now? Hopefully, a bit inflated, and loving every second of it. There's nothing wrong with self-confidence. It's okay to pat yourself on the back now and again and say, "Wow, I'm something special."

Let me explain why self-acknowledgment and self-love are

so important. Once I was coaching a young girl in her mid-20s, who was in a bad relationship. When I asked her why she stays with this man, she replied, "Because I don't think I deserve better. I'm just not good enough." Those were her exact words, and she really did believe them. But I didn't. I saw a beautiful woman with a kind heart and an ambitious spirit, but all she saw was an ugly duckling lucky enough to have found someone—even a jerk—to be with.

Self-confidence would have freed her from this man and set her on a path to finding a Great Man—someone who would have recognized her for the prize that she is, and treated her with respect and love. This is what I want for you—and for every woman out there. It's attainable, if you build your self-confidence. Just do the inner work. You will reap the rewards you deserve.

So let me ask you again: What makes you a *great* woman? Why do you deserve to be loved, honored, and cherished? Say it aloud. Now write it down. Commit it to memory and live by it. A Great Man will be glad you did. And so will you.

NOT JUST ANY MAN

You now know that you're a pretty incredible woman—check. And you now know the first step in meeting a man: Face your fears and leave the house—check. Now it's time to take it up a notch: It's time to learn *how* to meet a Great Man.

The way to meet a Great Man is to first decide what your vision of a Great Man is, and then secondly, to think and act like him. I know, I know, you're a *girl*. You're wondering how in the world can I expect you to think and act like a man, much less a *Great Man*. It's easy if you follow my step-by-step instructions.

ONE STEP AT A TIME

STEP 1: Do the prep work. It's time to create your Great Man. Is he tall, dark and handsome? Or is he short, stocky and lovable? Your preferences are your preferences. It's completely up to you. I want you to look deep within yourself and decide exactly what you want in a man and write it down.

"Why should I take the time to write it down when I already know it in my head?" Because I said so, that's why! I'm just kidding. I'm not going to *mother* you, I'm going to *train* you, and as your coach, I expect you to follow my instructions to the letter. This may sound harsh, but it's the only way this will work. And I assure you–this *will* work.

So let's try this again. "Why should I take the time to write it down when I already know it in my head?" Great question! I want you to do it because I believe you're more likely to get what you want just by writing it down. You'll have a list you can refer to again and again, should you ever find yourself straying from the powerful vision you first had of your Great Man. It's that simple and it's proven to work. Here's an example to help you hone in on what you're looking for in a man.

GREAT MAN WORKSHEET (EXAMPLE)

Age	35–55
Height	5'11"–6'3" He can be shorter if he's really hot, but not less than 5'8".
Weight	Proportional to his height. Not thin and not too heavy—just right.
Build	Tall, lean and athletic. No bodybuilders and no fatties.
Eyes	No color preference. Sultry and symmetrical.
Hair	Yes. No bald men, unless they're Bruce Willis!
Marital Status	Single or divorced. Not married!! I repeat, NOT MARRIED.
Children	Preferably none, but it's not a deal breaker.
Family	Big or small is okay. No family feuds.
Religion	Open. No fanatics.
Education	Highly educated or entrepreneurial. Intelligence is a must.
Profession	Fulfilled. He must love what he does. No workaholics.

Financial Status	Stable. Who am I kidding? Trump, are you single again?
Hobbies	Travel. Let's see the world together. You can golf in your next life.
Personality	Fun. Confident. Romantic. Honest. Dependable. Jerks need not apply.
Baggage	If it's packed neatly in a Louis Vuitton suitcase, it's okay. No duffle bags.
Bad Habits	He can smoke and drink, he just can't lie, cheat or steal.
Deal Breakers	Drugs. Lies. Treating me with anything less than total respect.
Comments	I want a handsome man who is successful and happy—a man who will treat me as good as I treat him, someone confident enough to be completely honest with me, no matter what the consequences. He doesn't have to be perfect, in fact I prefer he have a few flaws—just like me.
My Oath	I promise not to settle for a man who doesn't meet my basic criteria, no matter how lonely I get. I deserve a Great Man and I will find him and once I do, I will appreciate him.
Signed	Jane Doe

Now it's your turn. Get a sheet of paper and write down exactly what your Great Man is made of. Be thorough and completely honest. This list is for your eyes only; no one's going to judge you. Not even you.

MAKING IT STICK

Step 2: Now I'm going to hold you hostage! You're not allowed to leave the house until you memorize your answers. It's not plausible for you to carry your list around with you *all* the time. What if you lost it? What if the dog ate it? So commit it to memory and live by it. This is what you're looking for. This is what your Mr. Right looks like. This is what you want, so don't you dare settle for less.

It's important that you stick to your ultimate goal of finding your Great Man, your Mr. Right, not wasting your time on Mr. Right *Now*. If you wrote, "no married men," I want you to live by this rule, even if you meet the greatest man in the world who happens to be married. And if you said, "no drug users," then no drug users it is, even if he's hot and slightly dangerous, which you find appealing.

This is what I mean by "thinking and acting like a man." If a man knows he doesn't want to date a woman with children, he will absolutely stay away from women with children. He's confident that he will meet an attractive woman who doesn't have children, so he'll pass on Ms. Wrong (for him!) and continue the search for Ms. Right. He's just that focused. Now, I'm not saying he won't *sleep* with Ms. Wrong, I'm just saying he won't date her seriously. Catch my drift?

Men don't settle—and neither should you. The big difference is they get to test-drive a lot more often than is considered socially acceptable for women. It's not fair, but it is what it is. A man can brag about being with one hundred women. We even give him a positive name. I believe the term is "playboy," as if what he's doing is oh-so- adorable. But if a woman tells a man she's been with one hundred men, she's history. Yes, there's a double standard in play, here. I say you should do as you please. Just don't advertise it.

MEN DATE UP

Men date up while women often date down. Look around you and you'll see what I'm talking about. At any given moment, a mediocre man will walk by with an attractive, accomplished woman on his arm. How does he do it? Is he rich? Maybe he is, but not necessarily. Is he great in bed? Let's hope so, for her sake, but I wouldn't bet on it. He is—in a word— available. Or so he claims!

Women fool themselves into believing there aren't many men—let me rephrase that, many *single* men—left. This misconception makes you latch on to the very first guy who comes along, without regard to his marital status and drug habit. When you think and act like a man, you do just the opposite. You believe your options are limitless and realize that you can afford to be choosy. You throw back the little fish and cast your line again, confident that you'll hook the big Kahuna.

Please don't get carried away with this step. I'm not suggesting you only date men who meet *all* of your criteria. If you did, you'd only have one date every decade or so. However, I do want you to be selective and to stick to your ideals. Go out with men who intrigue you, and

MAN WANTED

Dear Jula,
I have one burning question: Where can I go to meet men?
Sienna

Dear Sienna,
That's a simple question with a not-so-simple answer. I'm asked this on a daily basis and the answer is always the same: They're *everywhere*. Men are all around us. They're at the grocery store, in our spinning class, at the gas station, sitting next to us on a plane . . . they're absolutely everywhere.

I know this is not the answer you were looking for. You want me to tell you a specific place to go, say Club Testosterone on Peachtree Street, but unfortunately there's no such club stacked with hot guys just waiting to meet you. And if there was, I'd hate to see the line to get in!

The best advice I can give you is to get out of the house as much as possible. He's out there, so always be prepared, approachable, and aware.
Jula Jane

move on when you realize they're not what you're looking for. Don't stay with the wrong man just to have a man in your life. This will backfire on you in the long run because you'll waste valuable years on the wrong guy when you should be enjoying life and searching for the Great Man.

NEEDY NO MORE

Step 3: Get a life. This is a piece of advice I'll repeat over and over throughout this book because it's so very important. Women who live a rich and rewarding life are so much more attractive than needy, clingy, boring women.

Whom would you rather date—a man who goes to work, comes home and looks to you to fulfill his needs, or a man who goes to the gym and to work, enjoys his friendships and hobbies, spends time with his family, and involves you in his balanced life? A secure woman will choose the latter, and will also recognize the importance of being equally engaging and engaged. And I'm not talking about a diamond ring, here!

Get a life that wows you so that when you meet a Great Man, you'll want to include him in it. Don't make the fatal error that so many women make: they swap their identity for his. He loves country music so all of a sudden, so does she. He likes to play golf, so does she. He's a Giants fan. . . . You get the point. In time, he'll lose interest and she will feel lost and empty. Be yourself and he'll love you for it.

Yes, think and act like a man. He doesn't sit by the phone waiting for you to call, and neither should you. He's busy building his career and hanging out with the guys. When his phone rings, he may answer it, or he may not. It depends on what he's doing at that moment. He'll get back to you when he can. And that's exactly what you should be doing—living your life and fitting him in. Don't cut off your girlfriend mid-sentence to answer a man's call. It's impolite and it makes you look desperate. Let her finish her thought and when time permits, give him a ring back. That's what a man would do.

A well-rounded man has hobbies and so should you. A man will choose to play a round of golf with his buddies and opt to see a woman later, while a woman will cancel her plans in order to spend time with a man. That's a *big* mistake. If he asks you out for dinner but you already have a yoga class scheduled, politely decline his invitation. Tell him why, then ask for a rain check. He'll understand and respect your response. If you value your time and interests, so will he. Most importantly, he'll value *you*.

A man makes his career a top priority. You do the same. Don't apologize for your busy schedule. He doesn't. And don't change your work schedule to suit him. He won't. And by all means, don't give up your career *ever* to please a man. He wouldn't do it for you.

Why is it men are permitted to be obsessed about their work,
but women are only permitted to be obsessed about men?
—Barbara Streisand

NO COMPROMISE

Step 4: Put yourself first. He does. I mean it. This is no time to compromise. Marriage is all about compromise. But dating isn't marriage.

I'm not suggesting you dig your heels in and throw a tantrum over little things. Not at all. I absolutely believe in give and take. I'm saying that you shouldn't compromise your principles. You never run the risk of losing a Great Man when you stick to your principles; it's when you compromise them that you're more likely to lose him.

For instance, if you're not comfortable having sex on the first date, then don't. Believe it or not, he'll be pleased that you didn't. Men are programmed to try to get you in bed from the moment they lay eyes on you. But this doesn't mean they want you to give in. Men enjoy the chase. That's why they love 'em and leave 'em so often. Once the chase is over, so is the fun.

Dear Jula,
I'm dating three men
and loving every
second of it. I
haven't committed
to any of them and
don't want to. Is
there anything
wrong with what I'm
doing? Some of my
friends and family
have voiced nega-
tive opinions. What
do you think?
Katharine

Dear Katharine,
I say, no harm, no
foul. You're not
cheating, you're ex-
ploring. There's no
shame in that, so
long as you're hon-
est. You don't have
to volunteer the in-
formation, but if
asked, you need to
come clean. Then
it's up to him to de-
cide if he'd like to
keep dating you or
not. As for those
judging you, don't
give them another
thought. This is your
life and you should
live it as you see fit.
Jula Jane

If a guy treats you in any way that's less than respectful, send him packing. Your principles make you who you are, so stand by them. When a girl disses (it's a word!) a guy, he moves on. Or he keeps coming back until he sleeps with her, and *then* he moves on. Why should you allow a man to treat you any differently than he expects to be treated? You shouldn't, so don't.

I THINK I CAN, I THINK I CAN

Step 5: Never give up. A Great Man pursues his dream job, his dream mate, and his dream life with unrelenting perseverance. He won't quit. He won't settle. And he won't lose hope. That's what I want for you. Don't settle. Don't quit. And don't lose hope.

If you always wanted to be a writer, pursue becoming a writer. Read lots. Take writing classes. And write! And if you fantasize about becoming a Pulitzer Prize-winning author, then you work your ass off to achieve that goal. Dreams are meant to be realized, so dream big, work hard and know that the only thing standing in your way is *you*.

This holds true for finding the love of your life. He's out there, but it's up to *you* to go after him. Nobody's going to deliver him to you on a silver platter. This would be nice, especially if he was dipped in Godiva chocolate (delicious!), but it's just not going to happen. It's up to you to *make* it happen.

This five-step exercise in thinking like a Great Man was tailored to retrain your thought processes. I no longer want you to think that he's out of your league. Instead, I want you to ask yourself, "Is he in *my* league?" Then grant him a few dates to find out. The power ball is in your court when you exude confidence (not arrogance), and go after what you want. Remember, you're a Great Woman who deserves a Great Man.

NEXT ORDER OF BUSINESS

Decide what you want in dating and love and go after it. This is a tall order and I fully expect you to take it seriously. I can't stand the thought of you dating haphazardly; you must know where you're going and how you're going to get there.

A lot of women waste their best years making mistakes and dating the wrong men, but not you. You're going to face this challenge head-on and take the next step towards a fun and fulfilling love life. Here's how.

PLAN OF ACTION

Write a love-life plan. I mean it. I want you to write it all down and not leave out a single detail. What kind of love life do you want? Do you want to get married and have children? Or would you rather date casually and enjoy brief relationships? Are you primarily focused on your career or is dating your priority? How do you plan to make it all

SO MANY MEN, SO LITTLE TIME

Dear Jula,
Life is good. I just finished a Fat Flush—I got a promotion at work, and I keep meeting great guys, one right after the other. My girlfriends complain that they can't meet any men, but I don't know what their problem is. We're going to the same places and I don't seem to have a problem. I'm having a ball, but they're starting to bring me down with their negativity. What can I do to stay on my high and still hang out with my friends?
Corinna

Dear Corinna,
I wouldn't change a thing. Your mojo is definitely working for you so don't rock the boat and don't let their bad vibes bring you down. Introduce your friends to the friends of the new men in your life and see what happens. Maybe they're just not as approachable as you are, so give them a hand. If they still give you a hard time, you may need to add some new, more supportive women to your posse. A true friend will encourage you, not pull you down.
Jula Jane

happen? A step-by-step love-life plan will answer these questions, so go ahead and write yours—not tomorrow or next week, but right now.

I know it's a daunting task, so I've made it simpler by giving you an example to go by. Curl up on the sofa with a cup of tea, pen and paper, and get to work. Just remember, this is only a basic guideline to get you started. I encourage you to add to it and go beyond it. The longer and more detailed your love-life plan, the better. This is the last piece of homework for a while, so make the most of it.

LOVE-LIFE PLAN (EXAMPLE)

What kind of love life do I want?	I want passion. I detest boredom and refuse to settle for anything less than stomach flips and sweaty palms. I want spontaneity and adventure. I want it all.
Do I want to get married?	I'm a die-hard romantic and love the idea of marriage, but I'm also a realist and question whether or not marriage will work for me. I'm undecided.
Do I want children?	So far, my clock doesn't seem to be ticking, or maybe I threw a blanket over it and can't hear it! I never say never, so maybe someday, but only under the right circumstances.
Do I just wanna have lots and lots of fun?	If I'm honest with myself, the answer is yes. I like the way a guy treats me in phase one of dating: he's attentive, romantic, fun, and sexually, well, he's my energizer bunny—he keeps going and going and going. I like all of that and am willing to forego the security of a long-term relationship in exchange for the excitement of a new one.
How do my career goals mesh with my personal ones?	My first priority is my work. I want to climb the corporate ladder and break through the glass ceiling. The man or men in my life will have to accept this, just as I am willing to accept that about them.

How do I plan to stay on track with my love-life plan?	I'm going to keep my heart in check and not let myself fall in love with the wrong man. I will make decisions that support what I truly want—free love.

This is a quick sample of a love-life plan. I want you to be as detailed as possible with yours and don't hold back. Again, this is for your eyes only, so speak the absolute truth. There is no right or wrong answer.

The underlying message is to love life. You now have an idea of what you want in love and when you obtain it, you will love your life even more.

I'M PROUD OF YOU

Let me say it once again: "I'm proud of you!" I really am. Most women go through life without a plan and wonder why they're not living their dream. Not you. No, ma'am. You took the bull by the horns (so to speak!) and did the work.

First, you took the initiative to buy a self-help book. Now you're reading it, and you're following its instructions step-by-step. A lot of women would have skipped the exercises and continued reading on, but not you. You recognize that in order to succeed you have to take direction and as a result, you not only have an outline of what a Great Man means to you, you've also drawn up a plan for welcoming him into your life—as a great woman. Congratulations! I'm proud of you.

Chapter Quiz

Do You Believe There's a Great Man Out There for You— or Are You Just Going to Settle?

1. When it comes to meeting men you:
   A. Sit at home and surf dating sites hoping to find a match.
   B. Are proactive—on dating sites, by networking and socializing, and by always being prepared and approachable.
   C. Have given up. All the good men are taken.

2. You're a woman who knows what she wants in a man—and you want:
   A. A quality man who is your equal and who inspires you to be the best that you can possibly be.
   B. Someone to come home to—any warm body will do.
   C. A sugar daddy.

3. Your three best assets are:
   A. Your boobs and your bum—technically that's three.
   B. Your job, your credit cards and your willingness to pay—sugar momma, anyone?
   C. Your charm, your kind heart and your willful spirit.

4. When you meet a man who doesn't meet your basic criteria you:
   A. Politely finish the conversation and move on.
   B. Latch on to him just in case someone better doesn't come along.
   C. Turn him down flat and act indignant that he dared to speak to you.

5. When you meet a man who is everything you've been searching for you:
    A. Suffocate him for fear of losing him.
    B. Play it cool and hope your game works to your favor.
    C. Win him over by being yourself—your best self.

6. You realize dating is a numbers game so you:
    A. Speed date any man who asks you out—Tom, Dick or Harry—it doesn't matter.
    B. Quit counting and quit dating—it's too much work.
    C. Go out with different men until you find the right man—a Great Man.

7. You live a full life and want a man who will:
    A. Give up his interests for yours.
    B. Complement it, not take away from it.
    C. Change *your* ways to *his* ways.

8. You have principles, and if a man asks you to compromise those principles you:
    A. Let him down easy and move on to a man who will respect you.
    B. Give in and give him what he wants.
    C. Grant him his wish and vow to be stronger the next time.

9. You've had disappointments and bad dates so you:
    A. Swear off men for good this time.
    B. Brush yourself off and remain positive—a Great Man is just around the corner.
    C. Cry yourself to sleep and man bash with your girlfriends.

10. You deserve a Great Man because:
    A. You're so hot.
    B. You've dated a lion's share of losers so your time has come.
    C. You're a Great Woman.

Your Results

You believe there's a Great Man for you
if you chose the following answers:

1. **B.** You don't wait around for things to happen, you make them happen. This will increase your chances of finding the right man—a Great man.

2. **A.** You will never settle for less than you deserve because you believe in yourself.

3. **C.** You are as beautiful on the inside as you are on the outside, and have the dates to prove it.

4. **A.** You will meet the man you're looking for sooner than later because you don't waste precious time dating men who are wrong for you.

5. **C.** You're something special and that's good enough for him.

6. **C.** You realize you have to kiss a lot of frogs to find your Prince Charming.

7. **B.** You're confident enough to do your own thing and willing to let a man be part of it—not replace it. That's a foundation for attracting a Great Man.

8. **A.** No man is worth sacrificing your principles—a motto which you live by. A Great Man will respect that.

9. **B.** You never give up, which means you will find a Great Man—it's only a matter of time.

10. **C.** Every Great Woman deserves a Great Man.

Congratulations! You're a Great Woman who believes there's a Great Man out there for you, and you're right—there is.

Chapter 2

If You Build It, He Will Come

Secret #2: You Must Become the Whole Package

*To put it bluntly, I seem to have a whole superstructure
with no foundation. But I'm working on the foundation.*
—Marilyn Monroe

This is a bit tongue and cheek, so let me lay it out for you. A man wants the whole package and nothing less. And when he finds it, he'll relinquish his little black book, say goodbye to his Days of Thunder, and finally seal the deal. And by that, I mean commitment, ladies. You heard me, *commitment*. Oh, how we love that word, as elusive as the actual concept might be. And why do we love it so much? Because it means no more competing with other women and better yet, it means we're one step closer to walking down the aisle.

We dream about marrying Prince Charming, from the time we're little girls in pigtails until the day we walk down the aisle dressed all in white, donning a Princess tiara. Oh, what a glorious day it will be, filled with wedding cake and flowers, presents, champagne and caviar. How sweet it is! Hold on! Not so fast. You still need the groom.

Planning your wedding before you're even engaged may be fun, but you're putting *way* too much pressure on yourself—and on him. It's time to toss out your *Bride Beautiful* magazines and get serious about becoming the best you can be— the whole package. Relax feminists; I'm not suggesting we change ourselves to land a husband. I'm saying we owe it to ourselves to get up from the sofa, turn off the television, and realize our full potential. Cinderella didn't go to the ball dressed in rags, and neither should you.

YOUR BEST SELF

Becoming your best self will not only make you more attractive to men, it will make you more attractive to yourself, and that's what's most important. Self-esteem is critical in seduction. Low self-esteem repels, confidence and self-sufficiency attract.

I know, I know, you're already the whole package, and if you really are, my hat's off to you. But before you skip to

NOT QUITE MARRIAGE MATERIAL

Dear Jula,
Excuse me if I sound arrogant, but I'm going to tell it like it is. I'm drop-dead gorgeous, a social butterfly, and quite a catch. I've been told that I'm a great kisser and a lot of fun. Why then am I still single? I'm 33 years old, perfect in so many ways, and yet I've never been asked to walk down the aisle. What's wrong with this picture?

Tiffany

Dear Tiffany,
You're scaring me. Take it down a notch, please. You may be pretty, but do you have depth? Is your favorite topic of conversation shopping, or can you competently discuss topics like politics and current events? I know you're fun to be around, but are you genuine? Are you nurturing? When the chips are down, do you stick it out, or do you hop on your boyfriend's jet and flit away? The verdict is

in: You're definitely date worthy; you're just not marriage material. Don't worry, there's a cure for what ails you, but it's going to require hard work on your part.

I want you to look in the mirror every morning and say this out loud three times: "Today, I will do something for someone else. I will learn something new and I will try very hard to become a better person." There now, that wasn't so hard, now was it? A wife should be her husband's best friend, his confidante, his rock, not just a pretty face. She should help him be a better man and welcome his love with an open heart. Is that you? The alternative is to stay focused on your looks and having fun, and to look for a man who simply wants a trophy wife. The choice is yours.

Jula Jane

the next chapter, ask yourself the following questions:

Am I financially secure? Am I physically fit and active? Is my image up to par? Am I a good cook? Am I well traveled? Am I fun? Am I happy? Am I emotionally stable? Am I a good conversationalist? Am I confident? I know this list may seem daunting, but don't get overwhelmed just yet. Take each question one step at a time.

I CAN BRING HOME THE BACON

First, focus on becoming financially secure. We become desperate and make bad decisions when faced with financial stress, so get your finances under control before anything else.

I'm not saying you have to become a millionaire, I'm merely suggesting that you should be able to pay your own bills and should not be drowning in debt. No one wants to take on another person's money problems and hearing a woman complain about her past-due accounts is an instant turn-off.

Have you ever overheard a friend chatting up a guy over a cocktail, telling him that she just filed bankruptcy and is losing her house? I have and it's not at all appealing. She may think she's just making conversation, but what she's really doing is sending the message that she's not good with money and that she's looking to be rescued.

Look at the big picture and take the steps needed to achieve financial security. If this means you have to work two jobs for a while and eat out less often, so be it. It's worth it.

When you have money in the bank and food on the table, you will relax and date wisely because you can afford to.

WORK YOUR BODY

You don't have to be a size 2 and a star athlete to be considered fit and active, but you do have to be able to walk to your mailbox and back without getting winded. Your overall weight is as important to your health as it is to attracting a man, and let me assure you, a healthy woman is a big turn-on.

Becoming your best self is just that, *your* best self, not someone else's ideal. Some women are thin while others are voluptuous. Both are equally beautiful. Please don't try to imitate what you see in Hollywood; it's too hard to live up to. Just be yourself, but again, be your *best* self.

Exercise, eat right, and find a hobby that keeps you moving—swimming, belly dancing, rollerblading, tennis, golf, mall walking, whatever it is that you enjoy. Just make it part of your lifestyle. And when you meet a man, don't give up your hobby for him, invite him to join you in your fun. Wow, you just became more desirable.

Speaking of working out, so many women complain about not being able to afford gym memberships, which is just an excuse to sit on the sofa and eat junk food. (I've been there!) You don't have to join an expensive gym to get in shape. Run Forrest, run! It's free. Grab your iPod or a good friend and pound the pavement. If running isn't your thing—perhaps you have bad knees—then stretch and do sit-ups in your living room.

Another common excuse is lack of time. Ladies, there's *always* time, it's lack of motivation that's the real deterrent. Dedicate just 20 minutes a day to some form of exercise. I understand you're exhausted from your hard day at work and the last thing you feel like doing is exercising, but it needs to be done. Take the dirty clothes off the treadmill; push it in front of the TV, if you must, and get moving. There's simply no excuse for not working out and staying healthy, especially when trying to land a man.

MIRROR, MIRROR ON THE WALL

Your image is a combination of your dress, your hair and makeup, and your overall grooming—your basic outward appearance. You have mere seconds to make a lasting impression, so make sure you always look your best. I really do mean *always*. Throwing on a cute outfit doesn't take any more effort than slipping on sweatpants and tennis shoes; it's the same amount of clothes, but one makes you look frumpy and lazy while the other says, "I respect myself."

"How do I know if I'm up-to-date or out of style?" That's easy: If you tease your hair, paint your nails red, and wear pantyhose with pumps, you're a leftover from the '80s. If you sport a sleek 'do, French nails, and let your

Dear Jula,
I have my eye on a really hot guy, but he's not pursuing me. I know you say that a woman should not chase a man, but how am I going to get a date with him if I don't make a move? I see him at least once every four to six weeks at various locations, strictly by chance. I tried to start a conversation a few times, but he always seems to make his escape before we bond. Is he not interested or is he just playing hard to get?

Amanda

Dear Amanda,
Men usually go after what they want. If he hasn't pursued you even after your attempts to let him know you exist, he probably has a girlfriend or is simply attracted to a different type of woman. You're probably Ms. Right, just not *his* Ms. Right. I'd let this one go and focus on meeting a man who adores you.

Jula Jane

gams go free, you're hangin' with the in-crowd.

If you don't know where to begin, enlist the help of friends and family. If that doesn't work, rely on professionals. Hire an image consultant, or ask for help at the beauty salon, and in clothing boutiques. They'll be only too happy to help.

This is a great time in your life to try something new. Cut your hair or get extensions. Go from brunette to blond (I do believe we really do have more fun!), or be daring and try red. You know what they say about redheads—hot, hot, *hot*. Take your mousy locks to a deep dark hue—something exotic. A new hairstyle is worth every penny and is just what you need to boost your confidence. Plan to go out with the girls that night and whenever you get your hair done. Looking your best will put you in a flirtatious mood.

I realize that maintaining your hair and nails can be tiresome and frankly, expensive, but think of the alternative—chipped nail polish and black roots! Yuck! If you have a limited budget, learn to give yourself manis and pedis at home. Just don't attempt to cut and color your own hair. Cut back on trips to the drive-through to save money for the hair salon. It's worth it.

See, when you break it down step-by-step, becoming your best self is not that complicated. You're now financially-secure (check), fit and active (check, check), and your new look is drop-dead gorgeous (check plus). Now it's time to get cooking!

I CAN FRY IT UP IN A PAN

Are you a good cook? "No, but I'm great at making reservations." That's all well and good, but have you ever heard the expression, "The way to a man's heart is through his stomach?" That means get in the kitchen, open up a cookbook, and teach yourself how to make at least one scrumptious meal.

So you say you can't boil water. So what! I can teach you. Get a pot. Fill it three-fourths full with cold water. Cover with a lid. Set it on the stove. Turn the knob to high. Now watch it boil. Caught ya! Lesson number one: A watched pot never boils. Leave the lid on and check on it periodically, and by periodically, I mean every few minutes.

Now that you can boil water, you can make pasta. Buy a box of angel hair pasta, which cooks quickly and tastes delicious, and follow the directions on the back. As for the sauce, buy something impressive in a jar. Can you say *Vodka sauce?* Pour it into a saucepan and let it simmer (that means low heat) while your pasta is cooking. In less than 15 minutes, you'll have prepared an impressive dinner for two. If you're feeling ambitious, toss a simple salad-in-a-bag and add some toasted French bread to thoroughly impress him. Bon appétit!

Becoming a good cook takes time and practice. Start out with simple meals like this one and gradually try more complicated dishes. Use friends as guinea pigs first. You don't want your first attempt at Beef Wellington and poached pears to go badly with a first date. Who needs that kind of pressure?

VIRTUAL GLOBE TROTTING

You don't have a silver spoon so how in the world can you become well-traveled? Be creative. You can fake it 'til you make it. Here's how.

Buy an atlas or go to a library and give yourself a geography lesson. Laugh all you want, but let's see how hard you're laughing when a guy asks you to go to Georgia and you say yes, thinking Atlanta and you find yourself far from home shivering along Russia's southern border. Oops.

Study your atlas until you're well-versed in locales of interest. Select five countries you'd like to visit and learn everything you can about them. Voila! You can now fake it.

"So Jennifer, have you traveled much?" "You know John; I'm completely obsessed with Dubai. I hear it's an amazing metropolis with great shopping and I hope to go very soon. How about you? Where was your last adventure?"

There's a whole lot of world out there and if you've limited yourself to your hometown and one trip across the border, you've got some traveling to do. It's so much fun to explore different cultures and ways of life, and having had these experiences makes you a lot more exciting to talk to.

LIFE OF THE PARTY

Conversation about exotic destinations is a perfect opportunity to show a man how much fun you are. Scope out your destination and suggest something thrilling. "How about a desert safari? You get a guided outing complete with dune bashing, sand boarding, camel riding followed by a belly dance show, henna painting and sheesha pipe smoking."

Men are explorers and want to have a good time. Let go of your fears and follow his lead. If he wants to take you white-water rafting, by all means, go. If he wants to take you skiing, get ready to slalom. And if he wants to go sky diving, go—but cheer him on from the side of the cliff. You're fun, but you're not crazy!

There are many ways to be a fun person. Be playful and lighthearted; don't take yourself too seriously. That doesn't mean you should be silly or obnoxious, simply easy- going. Laugh out loud, try new things, and smile a lot. Now that's fun.

PUT ON A HAPPY FACE

You're getting close to completing the list and turning yourself into a highly- sought after woman, but let's not forget just being happy. There's no place in this short life for negativity, so as that popular ditty goes, "Don't worry, be happy." Men want to be around happy women so if you want to become a man magnet, you need to put on a happy face. And guess what—there's an added bonus to this secret: Pretending to be happy will actually make you feel happy.

I bet you're wondering what's wrong with being yourself and letting your true, sorrowful feelings show. In the dating world, it's suicide. Men are problem solvers and if you're continually plagued with problems, a man is going to feel like a failure around you because after all, he can't solve your problems. In time, he'll move on to a happy woman who makes him feel adequate. It may seem unfair but it's true.

The fastest road to happiness is to . . . get a life. (Remember, I said this would come up repeatedly!) Fill your free time with exciting things to do and you won't have time to be unhappy. You'll be too busy having the time of your life—everyday! Your man will be relieved that he doesn't have to be your everything; he can be your something special, instead.

BEAUTIFUL NOT BATTY

Dear Jula,
I'm recently divorced, fiftyish and terrified about being on the dating scene with all of these fabulous looking, younger women. Where do I start?
Sandra

Dear Sandra,
The most important thing to do is to put these other women out of your mind. Remember, everyone has faults and flaws, no matter how beautiful or how young they are. And frankly, an older woman is a lot more mature and relatable than a 20-year old Barbie doll.
You need to focus on being the best that you can be, physically, emotionally, and financially. Once you do that, your confidence will be high and you will attract a quality man worthy of you.
Jula Jane

Women are, by nature, more emotional than men. This is just a fact of life. It's when our heads start spinning around and things go flying across the room that we need to stop and take stock in our emotions.

All men want their women to have a feisty way about them—just not *too* feisty. If you find yourself crying over spilt milk, or screaming at the waiter because he got your order wrong, it may be time to relax and get a grip. The tricky part is finding a nice balance between *calm* and *fiery*. Test the waters with your new man, erring on the calm side until you know his personality. If he likes passion and sparks, give it to him, but if he prefers a pussy cat, be sweet and coy.

Jealousy definitely falls under the category of emotional instability. Showing slight signs of jealousy can be flirtatious; just don't let it get out of hand. Lashing out at a guy because he looked in the general direction of another woman or storming out of a restaurant because his ex walked in is too much. You'll be labeled "psycho" and before you know it, he'll be back with his ex, because he'll reason, at least she's sane. Don't sweat the small stuff. It simply isn't that important and believe me, you're not impressing anyone with your drama.

CLIMB EVERY MOUNTAIN

If you are confident, you will attract not only one man, but *most* men. Confidence is powerful. It's seductive and it's a must if you plan to date. Build your confidence and he will come. In fact, he will flock. Building confidence is easier said than done, but it can be done. All you have to do is try: try to see the strength within you, try to face your fears, and try to be better than you were yesterday. When you strive for greatness, you assume greatness.

THE WHOLE PACKAGE

Now that you've checked off all of these necessary traits to becoming your best self, it's time to spice up even more. So, did you say yes to all of these questions? Great! You're well on your way to building your best self, but don't stop there. There's always something else that can be done to spice you up. Take salsa lessons or learn a new language. Volunteer with a worthy charity. Who knows, maybe you'll meet a handsome stranger while you're doling out meals at the soup kitchen.

Yes, your ultimate goal is to meet a man, but it's important to focus on you for a while. Find joy in your friends and family, and in your work and hobbies. Strive to be the absolute best that you can be, and truly learn to be content on your own. I can't express this enough. Respect and love yourself first and with conviction. Have confidence in your appearance, challenge your mind, and continue to grow as an individual.

Once you do, you'll say goodbye to lonely nights and solo dinners forever, because a man worthy of you will finally appear. It's not that he didn't exist before. He did. In fact, he's been waiting for you for quite some time. But you just weren't ready for him. Now, you are. If you become the "whole package," you'll be beating men off with a stick, or in your case, a sexy Jimmy Choo. Remember—if you build it, he will come.

Chapter Quiz

Are You the Whole Package, or Is There Something Missing?

1. Your idea of being financially secure is:
   A. Living paycheck to paycheck and letting men pick up the tab for you.
   B. Money in the bank, no revolving debt and an advancing career.
   C. Being married to a man who takes care of you.

2. Physically fit and active to you means:
   A. Being able to button your jeans while sucking in.
   B. Not important. He should love you just the way you are.
   C. Maintaining your ideal weight and exercising regularly.

3. An up-to-par image is:
   A. Age appropriate, fashion forward and fitting to your personality and circumstances.
   B. Clean clothes, brushed teeth and hair, and no chips in your fingernail polish.
   C. Whatever your mood dictates.

4. To be a good cook you need to:
   A. Know how to make reservations and order pizza.
   B. Try new recipes and not be afraid to make mistakes.
   C. Learn how to use a microwave. Ding—it's ready.

5. A well-traveled woman:
   A. Has explored other countries and continues to do so.
   B. Crosses the border now and again.
   C. Lives vicariously through the Travel Channel.

6. Your idea of being fun is:
   A. Making fun of people and laughing at your own jokes.
   B. Going along for the ride.
   C. Having a good sense of humor and an adventurous spirit.

7. Happiness is:
   A. Living your best life now.
   B. Hearing his voice after waiting days for his call.
   C. Fitting into your skinny jeans.

8. An emotionally-stable woman:
   A. Goes into a jealous rage when the waitress smiles at her date.
   B. Is cool, calm and collected in any given situation.
   C. Sits outside a boyfriend's house at all hours of the night hoping to catch him doing something wrong.

9. To be a good conversationalist:
   A. You listen more than you talk, and you pay attention to what the other person says, interjecting relevant thoughts.
   B. You wait for your chance to talk and then run on at the mouth.
   C. You speak only when spoken to and never interrupt.

10. A confident woman:
   A. Isn't afraid to show a little skin.
   B. Vies for attention.
   C. Knows her worth and lets others shine.

Your Results

You are the whole package
if you chose the following answers:

1. **B.** You are an independent woman who understands the importance of being able to take care of herself financially. You can survive with or without a man because you have the means to do so. This will allow you to choose someone you want instead of someone you need.

2. **C.** Your health is as important to you as your figure, so you work on both by eating right and exercising regularly. This is an attractive quality that will draw men to you.

3. **A.** You will always make a good first impression because you understand the importance of being appropriate and looking your best in any given situation.

4. **B.** You will never go hungry nor will you ever have a lack of male companionship because you're not afraid to experiment in the kitchen.

5. **A.** You will be the center of attention when telling tales of your international explorations. Every man will hope to be your next travel companion.

6. **C.** Men enjoy being with you because you don't take yourself too seriously and you're up for new and exciting things—with them.

7. **A.** There's no time like the present to enjoy all that life has to offer—so you do, and that's an incredible trait.

8. **B.** You never let them see you sweat and they respect that about you.

9. **A.** Both men and women enjoy your company because you listen to what they have to say, and are genuinely engaged in the conversation.

10. **C.** Your presence is enough to make any man melt.

Congratulations—you're the whole package! Make sure he deserves you.

Chapter 3

Lessons We First Learned in Kindergarten

Secret #3: You Must Always Mind Your Manners

We teach people how to treat us.
—Dr. Phil McGraw

Let's see, Kindergarten. What did I learn in kindergarten? Ah yes, I learned to play nice with others, to share my toys, to keep my hands to myself and to color within the lines. I also mastered my ABC's and my 123's. The most important thing I learned, however, was to mind my manners.

I learned very quickly that when I said please, as in, "Can I have a cookie, please," I was usually granted my request. And when I said, "Thank you," as in, "Thank you for this yummy cookie," I always received praise for being such a polite young lady. Please and thank you, that's easy. What else?

Ah, May I! Just when I thought I was doing so well, I learned I had been saying it all wrong. It's not, "Can I have a cookie," it's "May I have a cookie?" This was a little trickier and at five, I couldn't say what I was really thinking: "Can I have a cookie? . . . May I have a cookie? . . . Who cares! Just give me the damn cookie!" I had to learn to say it *their* way in order to get *my* way. "May I have a cookie, please? Thank you."

This was the first of many lessons I learned in Kindergarten and throughout my upbringing, and I'm thankful for every last one of them. Minding my P's and Q's has helped me stand out in a competitive business world—and in the cutthroat dating world. And it will help you, too. Here's how.

WHO, WHAT, WHEN, WHERE AND MOST IMPORTANTLY, WHY

Polished manners and proper grammar are critical, if you're going to date successfully. You have one chance to make a good first impression. So it's very important to always be "on" and composed. No matter where you are, who you're with, or what you're doing, you are on display and being judged, so always be polite and respectful, even when someone else is not.

For example, snapping at a waiter, even if he deserves it, will turn off the handsome gentleman who's been eyeing you all night. Instead of sending a drink over to your table, he'll turn his attention to someone else—the well-mannered woman who's been the model of decorum. Suddenly, Ms. Manners will be sipping *your* martini and smiling at the hunk who could have been *your* man, all because you weren't polite to your waiter.

How you treat others is a tell-tale sign of how you will treat your mate. If you're kind and considerate to strangers, then you're more likely to be kind and considerate to someone you love. And if you're rude and selfish towards people, then it's assumed you'll be self-centered and discourteous in a relationship. This may not always be true, but you are certainly going to be judged this way.

Now that you recognize how important good manners are to your social life, let's work on improving them. Anyone can be kind, considerate and respectful. It doesn't take money nor does it require an inherent skill; it simply takes the will to do it. There are no excuses for bad manners. This warrants repeating: There are no excuses for bad manners. If you're the type to fly off the handle over minor inconveniences and at the slightest perceived offense, changing your ways is going to take a lot of effort on your part, but it will pay off.

WITH COMPLIMENTS

Choose your words carefully every time you open your mouth, especially when on a date, or when chatting with a man who you might want to date. There are certain things you can say to turn a man on—and certain things you can say to turn him off. Let's focus on turning him on, shall we?

Sincere compliments, such as, "You smell great, what cologne are you wearing?" go a long way. That's a genuine statement (unless he just came from the gym) and will endear you to him. And when you tell a man, "I really like your tie. You have great taste," he hears that you like him, and is more likely to return the feelings. These positive, non-threatening comments break the ice and make him want to be around you. Everyone likes receiving compliments, so use it to your advantage, but remember not to overdo it.

Many women believe talking about sex with a man is a turn-on when, actually, it's a turn-off, a very big one, in fact. Present yourself as a lady and he will treat you as a lady. Come off as a floozy and he will, undoubtedly, treat you like a floozy. Keep it clean, ladies! Leave the dirty talk for the bedroom. If you want to seduce him, seduce him with compliments and witty conversation—now *that's* sexy.

IF YOU CAN'T SAY SOMETHING NICE ...

"Your mom is so skinny, she swallowed an M & M and looked nine months pregnant." "Oh yeah, well, you're a poohpooh head and uh, *your* mom looks pregnant." Rule number one: If you can't say something nice, don't say anything at all. Rule number two: If you don't have a good comeback, just walk away.

"I'm rubber and you're glue, what you say bounces off me and sticks to you." This nursery school rhyme has a nice ring to it, but it's not always true. A lot of people *are* affected by what others say to them or about them. If you're used to snapping at people when you're under pressure, or you speak to those in a lower position or class in a condescending manner, then it's time to realize that this is not okay. What you're doing is hurtful and viewed negatively. Contrary to what many people believe, treating people as if they're beneath you doesn't make you look important, it makes you look stupid.

Everyone deserves your respect, whether you think they do or not: The telemarketer who just interrupted your favorite episode of *American Idol* . . . the hostess who can't seat you right away because there are ten people ahead of you . . . the bathroom attendant at your local bar. She's doing the best she can. It's not her fault the woman before you peed on the seat and used the last bit of TP. If you gave her a chance, she would have checked the stall and tidied up before you took your turn.

What does this have to do with dating secrets? A lot! What if your

VERBAL ABUSE

Dear Jula,
I'm in a relationship with a verbally-abusive man and I don't know how to get out. He tears me down every day with ego-blowing comments. My self-esteem is so low; I'm beginning to believe what he says. Maybe I won't find a man who's better, and maybe I won't be able to find a job to support myself. Could he be right? Should I just suck it up and stay with him?

Carmen

Dear Carmen,
He's beating you down to make you weak so he can control you. If you give up, he wins. My guess is that he's extremely insecure and feels better about himself when he brings you down. He's afraid you'll leave him one day, so he's trying to make you feel like you can't make it without him. It's sick and it won't stop unless you do something about it.

If you love him and want to stay with him, you're going to have to get help. If he's not willing to address the problem and work on it, you have no choice but to leave him. You deserve to be happy and despite what he says, you will find someone better, and you *will* find a job. You just have to find the strength to make a move.

Jula Jane

boyfriend worked as a telemarketer to put himself through college and he overheard you reaming an innocent caller? His opinion of you would sour just a bit, perhaps indefinitely. This behavior might not necessarily be a deal-breaker, but it certainly won't win you any points. And what if the hostess you snapped at turns out to be the sister of your next blind date? Remembering how rudely you treated her, she'll put the kibosh on your new romance.

You're thinking, "I get it, but why should I worry about the bathroom attendant? How is my bathroom behavior ever going to come back to haunt me?" In more ways than you can imagine. For instance, your boyfriend's ex-girlfriend happens to be behind closed stall doors in the bathroom and overhears you making fun of the attendant with your girlfriends. I assure you; her next move is to beeline it for your man to let him know how mean you are to those less fortunate. He won't break up with you, but he will find your behavior distasteful. I saw this happen once with my own prying eyes. The bottom line: Be nice, be nice, be nice.

CHIVALRY'S DEAD

Dear Jula,
Is it too much to ask for my boyfriend to open the door for me, or for him to give me his seat at the bar? What happened to the days when men were gentlemen and women were ladies?
Anne Marie

Dear Anne Marie,
No, it's not too much to ask. A man should show a woman respect and be courteous, especially a man she's dating. There are gentle ways to mend his ways, without coming across as demanding.

For starters, stop opening your own door. When you pull into a parking space and he leaps out, stay put. Wait for him to come to your side and open the door.

ROOM FOR IMPROVEMENT

I recently noticed my own behavior towards others was slipping. I was short with service people, quick-tempered when I didn't get the table I wanted, and even rude to a telemarketer. My loving fiancé brought it to my attention, much to my embarrassment. Even though I turned the tables and made him feel badly for criticizing me, deep down I knew he was right. I just didn't want to admit it.

When you approach an entrance, stand to the side so he can reach the handle. Keep this up and he'll treat you like the lady you've shown yourself to be.

As for not giving you his seat at the bar, there's a great way to fix that. Stand by your comfortably seated man until a stool opens up somewhere else—hopefully, next to a hot guy. Kiss your man on the forehead, turn and walk away with no explanation. Watch how fast he gets up from his throne to be by your side. If he complains, simply tell him your feet hurt and you wanted to be more comfortable. He can't argue with that. Do this every time and before you know it, he'll jump at the chance to give you his seat.

Jula Jane

The truth was I was being rude to people who didn't deserve it. I couldn't understand why. I was fairly content with my life. Why, then, had I mistreated so many people? In the end, I decided I really didn't have a reason; I was just being insensitive.

I knew it was time to get back to the real Jula Jane. I decided from that moment on to always be the easy-going and accommodating woman I once knew. The table I want is taken, so what? I'll take the next best thing or wait until it *is* available. I paid for a first-class plane ticket but got bumped back to coach—oh well. At least I have a ride home. It's this new attitude that makes people more attracted to me and me to myself. As a result, I feel so much better.

Make the following five courtesies part of your daily life and you, too, will walk around with a smile instead of a wrinkle-causing frown. If nothing else, you'll save a fortune on Botox.

1. **Think before you speak.** Take a breath, smile and then speak. Don't lash out. Address everyone politely and respectfully, no matter what. Be firm when necessary, but never curt.

2. **Treat everyone how you wish to be treated.** Do you ever want to be yelled at or talked down to? I doubt it, so don't do it to anyone else. If you like being told "please" and "thank you," say "please" and "thank you" every time it's called for, and even when it's not. There's no such thing as being too polite.

3. **Open doors for people.** Allow others to get on and off the elevator before you, offer older people and women with babies your seat, and if someone cuts in line, let them—or calmly let them know they accidentally stepped in front of you.

4. **Help others whenever possible.** If you see someone struggling to retrieve a can from a high shelf at the grocery store, help them. When a man in a wheelchair approaches a door, open it for him with a smile. And if another woman is interested in the last pair of black patent leather Manolo Blahnik shoes on the size 8½ sales rack, offer to let her have them. (If she's as polite as you, she'll insist that you take them, instead.)

5. **Use compliments.** "You look great today . . . I love that dress. Where did you get it?" It's so easy to brighten someone's day with a few simple words. Their natural reaction will be to return the compliment. "Thanks, your shoes are stunning. Are they Jimmy Choos?" Win-win. You both come out beaming.

ROAD RAGE

I may not have had a driver's license or a car in Kindergarten, but I did have the fastest Big Wheel tricycle in class. It was fire-engine red with one big impressive wheel in the front and two smaller ones in the rear. I was like lightning, turning corners and turning heads—until road rage took over.

I was spinning out of control, bumping Tikes off the playground and tailgating like nobody's business. I always had to be first—at any cost. I finally saw the error of my ways just as I pushed past Susie in her pink Barbie dream convertible and plowed into little Johnny pedaling his classic wooden red ride 'em car. Our wheels were totaled and my pride was bruised. I felt terrible about running into him, but fortunately, nobody got hurt. That was it for me. I hung up my driving shoes and vowed never to get behind the wheel of a Big Wheel again.

How about you? Has road rage ever gotten the best of you? I bet there's not a single person reading this book who hasn't flipped another driver the bird, or cursed at someone who cut them off. When you're stressed out, tired, and just want to get home, traffic can get the best of you.

But remember, you are responsible for your actions behind the wheel. You do not become invisible once you shut your car door and put the key in the ignition. Everyone can still see you. They can see you singing along with the radio, applying lipstick, and talking on your cell phone. And they can see your obscene gestures.

You may be thinking, "Who cares, I'm never going to see them again." Not so fast. You are bound to run into people you know and who know you, while driving to work or on the way to the mall, regardless of the size of your city. Tailgating your boss may not go over so well, and giving the finger to the man who took you out last night but accidentally cut you off this morning, will, in all likelihood, fail to lead to another date. So be on your best behavior.

What's a girl in a hurry to do? Roll down the windows and smell the roses. In other words, *relax!* Getting upset and cursing at other drivers won't get you where you're going any faster; it'll only drive your blood pressure up, turn your face

Dear Jula,
Why do men have to be in charge of the television remote? My boyfriend practically hyperventilates when I have it. He can change the channel while I'm watching something, but if I do that to him—look out! I don't think it's fair. How can I win the battle for the remote control?
Debra

Dear Debra,

You can't. Let this one go. Television is important to a lot of men and obviously, it's of great importance to your man. Grant him the power to control the remote and you will win his heart. If you're dead set on watching *Dancing with the Stars,* record it and watch it later, or let him know how much you want to see it and go into another room. He probably would rather sit through your program with you by his side rather than watch his show all alone. Men are softies when we put their needs first. Give it a try.
Jula Jane

red, and make you look silly. Here are five polite ways to re-
duce road rage and impress those around you, including your
Great Man.

1. **Share the road.** Allow someone driving faster than you to
   get in front of you. Don't speed up when you realize
   they're trying to pass. We all travel at different speeds;
   don't take it personally. And when you see someone desperately trying to merge, let them. Frankly, it's dangerous
   not to.

2. **Give up a space.** Have you seen two cars battle it out
   over one spot, neither willing to budge? It's pathetic. If
   you approach a parking spot at the same time as another
   car, be the bigger woman and let her take it. It's not
   worth the fight.

3. **Don't honk your horn at anyone.** So the guy in front of you
   fell asleep at the wheel and the light just turned green—
   get over it. He'll wake up in a second, if not on his own vo-
   lition, then because of the sound of the *other* cars honk-
   ing impatiently. We've all done this, so cut him some
   slack.

4. **Never engage in a road rage race.** This is when one car
   cuts off another car and the offended car chases after it,
   relentlessly trying to regain its lead status. This can go on
   for miles, endangering everyone in the vicinity. Won't you
   feel stupid when you finally catch up and realize the person in the offending car is your boyfriend's mother? Oops!

5. **Be polite in traffic jams.** We all have places to go, people
   to see, and things to do, and though (in your mind), your
   mission is way more important to mankind than that of the
   drivers around you, it just might not be. What if the car you
   refused to let over was driven by a doctor on his way to
   deliver a baby? Or the car you caused to run into the

ditch carried a mother and her three children? Would knowing this have made you act differently, more politely? Assume everyone's mission is as important, or maybe even more important, than your own, and act accordingly.

The moral of this story is quite simple: Do unto others as you would have them do unto you. If you want to stand out in the dating world, be polite, control your emotions, and learn how to correctly read body language. Make good manners part of your lifestyle, not just while you're on a date, but all day, *every* day—at work, at home, at play, and everywhere in between. Now, I know it may not be easy to live by this dictum, but here's an incentive: When you do something nice for someone else, it makes you *feel* good and it makes you *look* good—to the man you want to be in your life, and to everyone around him. Polished manners attract polished men.

Chapter Quiz

Shall I Call You
Miss Manners or Miss Faux Pas?

1. When an elevator door opens you:
   A. Are the first one on and the first one off.
   B. Stand to the side and allow others to exit before you enter.
   C. Push past people thinking, "the last one in is a rotten egg."

2. If your waiter screws up your order you:
   A. Politely let him know and wait patiently for him to correct his mistake.
   B. Eat most of the unordered meal and then send it back in a huff, refusing to pay.
   C. Leave him a penny for a tip to teach him a lesson.

3. In traffic you:
   A. Embrace the motto "every man for himself."
   B. Allow cars to merge, don't tailgate and treat others as you yourself wish to be treated.
   C. Let road rage get the best of you.

4. When a man offers to buy you a drink you:
   A. Order an expensive glass of wine then leave him standing there by himself.
   B. Look at him like he's lost his mind and walk off.
   C. Thank him for the offer, and either decline politely, or accept and spend some time talking to him—while you sip his offering.

5. If you decide to cancel a date you:
   A. Call him as far in advance as possible and let him know that you've changed your mind about going out with him.
   B. Simply don't show up—he'll get the picture.
   C. Send him a quick text message and avoid all contact.

6. While on a date you realize that this guy is not for you, so you:
   A. Sneak out while he's in the men's room.
   B. Finish the date and if he calls you again, you kindly let him know that you think he's a great guy, but he's just not for you.
   C. Order something really expensive and flirt with the hot waiter.

7. When a man gets a little too fresh you:
   A. Slap him across the face and storm out.
   B. Let him know that he's going faster than you'd like and give him a second chance.
   C. Let him do whatever he wants because you're too timid to speak your mind.

8. You and your best friend spot a hot guy in a crowded bar. You:
   A. Let her have him. She's prettier and has a better chance of winning him over.
   B. Fight over him as if he's the last man on earth.
   C. Let her know that you're interested in meeting him and ask her to sit this one out. If she declines, you play her for him—rock, paper, scissors—and it's settled.

9. While on a date you meet someone more interesting. You:
   A. Ditch bachelor #1 and hook up with bachelor #2.
   B. Do nothing and hope to cross paths in the future.
   C. Slip him your business card, wink at him and tell him to call you.

10. When a man in a bar acts obnoxious towards you, you:
    A. Simply walk away and if he follows, you tell him in a direct manner to leave you alone.
    B. Cause a big scene and enjoy the attention it brings.
    C. Put up with it because you aren't strong enough to stop him.

Your Results

I'll crown you Miss Manners
if you chose the following answers:

1. **B.** You are aware of other people around you and treat them graciously, which makes you stand out in a crowd.

2. **A.** You recognize that people are human and make mistakes and respond with patience. This is a charming trait.

3. **B.** You share the road and play nice with others, which means you'll play nice with men too. That will put him at ease.

4. **C.** You understand how hard it is for a man to approach a woman and show kindness, whether you're interested in him or not. Everyone will notice and respect you for it.

5. **A.** You appreciate a man's interest, even if you don't share his feelings. Good karma will follow you.

6. **B.** You honor your word and speak the truth, which will leave a positive impression on everyone you meet.

7. **B.** He's overcome by your beauty and can't help himself—who can blame him? You are confident enough to set boundaries and stand by them—now that's hot.

8. **C.** You are a gracious woman, who goes after what she wants. Men love that.

9. **B.** Being a polite woman, you stay focused on your date and in return, your date stays focused on you.

10. **A.** You're nice until it's time not to be nice—then you're firm and that's hard to resist.

Chapter 4

Dating 101

Secret #4: Date to Play the Field, Not to Play House

It is the woman who chooses the man
who will choose her.
—Unknown

I've always thought you should "try on" or date as many men as you wish before settling on just one. That is, after all, what dating is all about—trying on different lifestyles and personalities until you find one that suits you to a T. You wouldn't buy a new dress without slipping it on first, now would you? So why should a man be any different?

Then again, who says you have to settle on just *one* man? You have a closet full of dresses, why not have a dance card full of men? Seriously, isn't it fun to wear a different dress each night of the week? And when you tire of a dress, isn't it fun to give it away and wear a new one? The same holds true with men. You can date a different man each night of the week and when you tire of one, you can give him away at a BYOB (Bring Your Old Boyfriend) party and get a new one!

DATING FOR FUN

Dating for fun means you aren't focused on the future; you're living in the moment and having the time of your life. When you date for fun, you don't have to be concerned about all the details. You can date whomever you want and not care if he has a pot to piss in, or not. Let's hope he has enough to pick up the check, but really, who cares? You're just using him for sex. Check, please.

I think women should do a lot more of this. Imagine, one night you're sipping champagne and eating caviar at the finest restaurant in town, accompanied by a distinguished older gentleman. The next night, you're sloshing a Cosmopolitan on the dance floor at a hip new nightclub, while learning some new moves from the twenty-something hottie you just met. Sounds good to me!

When you date for fun, you set your own schedule, make your own rules, and answer to no one. You do whatever pleases you and you don't feel guilty about doing so. You live life one glorious minute to the next, never knowing what lies ahead—a quick trip to Tahiti or perhaps cocktails aboard a yacht. The possibilities are endless.

DATING FOR THE FUTURE

On the other hand, for some, it may be wiser to not waste valuable time on men who aren't marriage material. You may feel you only have so many man-landing, child-bearing years left, so it's better to stay on target—land a man, bear his children.

When you date with your future in mind, you have to have a plan. Reflect back on Chapter 1 and your love-life plan; this will serve as your guide.

> *Whenever I date a guy, I think,*
> *"Is this the man I want my children*
> *to spend their weekends with?"*
> —Rita Rudner

Planning for your future changes the way you date. Instead of lying under the stars with a starving artist, you hang out at Biff's parents' summerhouse. You focus on Biff's education, upbringing, genes, career ambitions, and all the responsible traits that come with a good husband. And you toss aside your starving artist. This might not be very romantic, but you feel it's the sensible thing to do.

You must know what you want and go after it. If you want to get married and have three children before you turn 35, then you should only date men who are single and who want children, otherwise you're just wasting your time. Why risk falling in love with someone who absolutely doesn't want children? You're not going to change his desire. You may change his *mind,* but not his *desire,* and that's not a good situation to bring a child into. Find someone who wants what you want and you'll be a lot happier.

Dear Sarah,
I'm not going to beat you up over this one, so long as you keep your promise to never let it happen again. Here's my diagnosis: You had a momentary lapse of sanity. Clearly, a sane person would never declare their love for a stranger, so you must have been insane.

I'm just kidding (a little). You just got caught up in the moment. You were thinking, "I love this guy's company," but your mouth said, "I love you." An honest mistake. You can try to salvage this one by explaining what happened, but for ego's sake, I'd move on.
Jula Jane

DATING FOR SECURITY

Though dating for fun is, well, fun, it's hardly a plan for security. Having one man in your life inherently brings with it a sense of security. You have someone to come home to, someone to rely on, and someone to grow old with, and that's not so bad. The thought of living your final years alone can be frightening, which is why having a significant other is so attractive. I'm not saying you have to get married to find security. Some of the best relationships don't involve a ring and an "I do," they just *do*.

Take Angelina Jolie and Brad Pitt, for example. They aren't married, yet they have had a child together and are raising three adopted children as well. When asked about their relationship, they voice great love and admiration for one another. They reportedly refuse to get married until same-sex marriages are legal. Is this a political statement, or a convenient excuse? It doesn't really matter. The point is that they're living a "married" life without the piece of paper, and so can you—if that's what you want. Another great example of love without marriage is the relationship between Goldie Hawn and Kurt Russell. They've been together for more than 20 years. That's longer than most marriages!

Keep in mind, dating a different swinging Richard every night isn't going to bring about financial security, unless he happens to be a philanthropic billionaire, the way a relationship and marriage will. Then again, who says you can't make your own money and establish financial security on your own? For that matter, who says you have to grow old with a man? Your best friend or sister may provide just as much companionship as a man would, maybe more. Your idea of security lies within your own ideals, not someone else's.

THEN COMES
BABY IN A BABY CARRIAGE

Most people believe you should get married before you have children. Do you feel you need to be married to have a baby? Do you even want a baby? If you do, then you need to date for the future. If you feel it's perfectly acceptable to have a baby out of wedlock and become a single mother, then you can date for fun. You don't need to be so consumed with finding the right husband. Instead, you can focus on other things, like how the hell you're going to pay for this baby on your own.

'TIL DEATH DO WE PART

With the divorce rate teetering around 50 percent, why is it we still believe in marriage? I'm beginning to think marriage is an antiquated concept. Can we really remain happy and in love and committed to one person until death do we part? I'd like to think so, but statistics say no. And since I'm questioning conventional wisdom, I might as well take it a step further: Is monogamy an outdated concept? Are we really supposed to believe that a man is capable of having sex with only one woman for the rest of his life? And are we to believe that a woman is capable of sleeping with the same man for the rest of her life—the one with the beer gut and no sense of romance? Conservative statistics estimate that 60 percent of men and 40 percent of women will be unfaithful, so maybe a future with marriage isn't all that it's cracked up to be. Maybe dating for fun, until death do you part, is the way to go. That's for you to decide. Relax. . . . You can make one decision today, and then change your mind later. That is, after all, a woman's prerogative.

NAVIGATING THE DATING SUPERHIGHWAY

Dating is a roller coaster ride, full of highs and lows, twists and turns. It can be frustrating, but it's also a lot of fun, and certainly, worth the anguish. But only if you do it well. Which brings me to my next lesson: I'm about to reveal what you should do and what you shouldn't do when on a date, what to wear, what to talk about, where to go, and when and how to call it a night, plus much, much more. This is Dating 101 and you're trying to earn an A, so open your mind and absorb what I'm about to share with you.

FIRST DATE DO'S AND DON'TS

In the business world, it's easier to get repeat business from an existing client than it is to land a brand new client. The same is true in the dating world. It's easier to get a second date with someone you've already gone out with, than it is to secure a date with a brand new guy. Plus, statistics show that men take just 15 minutes to decide if they want to go out on a second date with a woman. (Women, on the other hand, mull over this decision for an hour.) That's why it's so very important to make a good first impression.

First date do's and don'ts are completely different from *fourth* date do's and don'ts, which are completely different from *tenth* date do's and don'ts, and so on and so on. How will a girl ever really know what's right and what's wrong? Trial and error, *that's* how.

First dates carry more weight, and as a result, tend to raise even more questions. For instance: Do I kiss him or don't I? I think you should never be too eager, especially when you're just getting to know a man. Never kiss on the first date. I mean it. I don't care if he's the hottest guy you've ever laid eyes on and you're overcome with lust. It's a bad idea. Leave him guessing as to whether or not you find him kissable. Wait at least three dates to let a man kiss you. This gives you time to get to know him and it allows the tension to build. Your first kiss will be explosive.

> *If you kiss on the first date and it's not right, then there will be no second date. Sometimes it's better to hold out and not kiss for a long time. I am a strong believer in kissing being very intimate, and the minute you kiss, the floodgates open for everything else.*
> —Jennifer Lopez

Once the kissing begins, keep it private. Never kiss in public, especially in a bar. This makes you look trashy. There are many free-spirited, sexually-charged women out there who feel they should be able to express their sexuality whenever and wherever they feel like it. I agree to a point, but PDAs (public displays of affection) just aren't appropriate when it makes others uncomfortable. Be respectful when locking lips in public, but do as you please in private.

Should I sleep with him, or not? I think you know what I'm going to say on this matter! Never, ever sleep with him on the first date. Try sleeping with a man on the first date and see what happens: He'll disappear so fast you'll get whiplash: "It was nice knowing you!" Try waiting to sleep with a man until say, the fourth date: "Last night was wonderful. I just had to call you this morning." Now, try waiting until you're in a committed relationship: "I want you to be my wife." Every action and reaction helps guide you on your subsequent dates.

DRESS FLIRTY, NOT SLUTTY

What you wear contributes tremendously to whether your first date is a success or a failure. You have one chance to make a lasting impression, so please put some thought into it. Find out where he's taking you and inquire about the dress code. (If you're too shy to ask him, contact the restaurant directly.) Slip on your best butt-enhancing jeans and a flirty top. I said, flirty, not slutty! Keep the cleavage to a minimum. A lot of women feel the need to wear low-cut attire in order to get attention, but not you. You know that this will divert his attention away from you (and onto a particular *part* of you!), and possibly give the wrong impression. This doesn't mean you should go backless, either. Keep the skin show to a minimum.

If the night calls for something dressier, go for a classic little black dress. It always works. Pair it with a striking scarf, sophisticated jewelry, killer pumps and a clutch, and you're set. This outfit will let him know you're confident and not afraid to be a lady. It will also show that you're comfortable relying on your charm and not your cleavage.

LET HIM PICK THE PLACE

I like to leave the location up to the guy because it gives me insight into his personality and his tastes. But if he asks you to make

DOUBLE BOOKING

Dear Jula,
I made plans to meet two different guys at a bar on the same Friday night, not knowing for sure if the first guy would actually show up. He did, and so did bachelor number two. I was definitely more interested in the first guy and basically blew off the other. He got angry and told me off. I think he's being unfair. Men double book and laugh it off. Why can't women?

Joanne

Dear Joanne,
Men may double book, but that doesn't mean women should. I get it, you're afraid the guy you're most interested in will stand you up, so you ask your second choice to meet you. It's not a nice thing to do. You run the risk of hurting someone because you're being selfish. Who knows, both guys may be date-worthy, but you won't know because you've turned one, if not both, of them off. Next time, ask a girlfriend to come with you. If your date shows, she can join you, and if he's a no-show, you have your girl there to help you score another date.
Jula Jane

a suggestion, respond with something unique and exotic, say a Middle-Eastern restaurant with belly dancing, and then encourage him to choose the next time.

There are a lot of great places to try out on a date, from casual to formal, from laid back to thrilling. Research your area and make a detailed list of restaurants, bars, lounges, theme parks, galleries, sporting events, etc. This way, you will always have something great to suggest when the occasion presents itself.

DECIDE HOW TO GET THERE

As nice as it is for a man to pick up a woman for their date, safety must come first. If you don't know him well, offer to meet him at the restaurant. It's unwise to let a stranger know where you live, plus you'll be happy you have your own car, should you decide to end the date early. Do be prompt; don't be fashionably late or uncomfortably early. If he says, "I'll pick you up at 8:00," be ready by 7:45. If he asks you to meet him at the restaurant around 7:00, arrive precisely at 7:00.

But if you're comfortable with this man, encourage him to pick you up. If he's the lazy type and insists on meeting you to save driving out of his way, politely cancel the date. If you don't warrant 30 minutes of his drive time, then he doesn't warrant three hours of your face time. Period.

BE CHATTY, BUT NOT A CHATTY CATHY

Talk about interesting things, like your passion for the arts or your love of photography, and then ask him about his

TOP 10 CONVERSATION DO'S

1. Do ask what he's passionate about
2. Do think before you speak
3. Do ask what he likes to do for fun
4. Do talk about your favorite food and wine
5. Do ask where he last vacationed
6. Do keep it about him
7. Do talk about electronics, sports, and music
8. Do stay positive
9. Do maintain eye contact
10. Do more listening than talking

interests. Keep the banter light and fun; please don't bring up politics or religion, or your ex. The top conversation-killer, according to a survey of 39,000 singles by the website, It's Just Lunch, is a past relationship. Nearly half found that topic difficult to digest.

The topic of conversation sets the mood for the date. Talk about sex and the date will lead to sex—at least, that's what *he'll* think. Talk about politics or religion, and the date will lead to a debate. Talk about your past relationships, and the date will lead to bitterness. Talk about something interesting and light and the date will lead to another date.

Dating is meant to be fun and flirty. Keep it that way. You're not planning a life together, nor are you conducting an interview. You're being in the moment. He doesn't need to know your blood type, or your mother's maiden name, and you don't need to know the name and weight of all of his ex-girlfriends. All you need to discover is whether or not you enjoy each other's company.

But don't monopolize the conversation. He'll get bored and lose interest. Let him do most of the talking and he'll think you're the best conversationalist he's ever met. The less you speak, the more intrigued he'll be. Women can chat with their

TOP 10 CONVERSATION DON'TS

1. Don't talk about an ex
2. Don't bring up sex
3. Don't focus on the future, stay in the moment
4. Don't debate politics
5. Don't discuss religion
6. Don't monopolize the conversation
7. Don't talk about your finances or his money
8. Don't be catty
9. Don't ask what kind of car he drives
10. Don't forget to breathe

girlfriends about everything—and nothing—for hours upon hours each day. Guys tend not to converse as much. In fact, men use about 12,000 words per day while women use about 25,000. That's more than twice as many words a day. Try to be aware of this female trait so you can control it. When you find yourself running at the mouth, simply close it. He won't notice; he tuned you out 5,000 words ago.

Give him that rare opportunity to just blab away. A skilled conversationalist will have an endless supply of dates, not because she has so many wonderful things to say, but because she makes her date feel wonderful just by being with her—because she listens. You'll be amazed at the effectiveness of this particular dating technique.

A foolish man tells a woman to stop talking, but a wise man tells her that her mouth is extremely beautiful when her lips are closed.
—Unknown

BODY TALK

Whether you like the sound of it or not, the truth is, when you're on a date, you are acting as a saleswoman. You're not

HOW TO TALK WITH YOUR BODY

1. **Use eye contact.** Look directly at him (but don't stare) when you speak and when you listen. Flirt a little with your sparkling eyes and fluttering eyelashes. If he won't make eye contact, something's wrong. He's either hiding something and/or isn't being very honest.

2. **Sit up tall and alert.** Less like the Queen's guard and more like Oprah. Lean forward ever so slightly towards him. This shows you're having a good time and are interested in what he's saying. If he's slumped in his chair and his eyes are everywhere but on you, he's not engaged and is looking for an exit strategy.

3. **Don't yawn.** Hold it in, swallow it, whatever you have to do. Just don't yawn. It says, "I'm bored because you're boring." And if your date lets out one yawn after the other, you're in trouble, because he's saying the same thing. Change the subject to something funny, or pay him a compliment, i.e., "I just noticed your big strong arms. Wow! Let's order another round of Mojitos."

4. **Get close to your date.** Don't smother him but get closer than you would to a friend. If he moves away, he's not that into you, but if he welcomes the affection, he's feeling it, too. An easy way to test this is to stroke his arm, just slightly, then pull away. If he responds by sweetly holding your hand, you know where his mind is—on you.

5. **Smile.** A warm smile and a gentle laugh will make him fall head-over-heels in love with you, or at the very least, *deeply* in like. According to a survey by the website It's Just Lunch, 53% of singles believe that a great smile is the single most attractive feature. And if he smiles back, he's yours!

selling a product, of course. You're selling yourself. On a date, you want to demonstrate that you're an honest, loyal, fun, and intelligent woman—and that he'd be lucky to be with you.

You are selling everything, from your personal likes and dislikes, to your attraction to him, to how much you like the restaurant he selected, to whether you find him interesting (or not), to the very idea of him spending a lifetime with you. That's a big job, so watch what you do! Notice, I didn't say watch what you *say*, I said watch what you *do*. Body language reveals a lot more about what we're thinking than we realize.

Most experts agree that it takes between 90 seconds and 4 minutes to decide if we're attracted to someone, and as much as we'd like to believe that the draw is the cute one-liner we're famous for, it actually isn't. More than 50 percent of our first impression of a person is derived from their body language, not from spoken language. And *what* we say isn't as important as *how* we say it. Nearly 40 percent of one's impression comes from the tone, speed and inflection of an individual's voice.

SPENDTHRIFT

Before you order, ask your date to recommend a dish from the menu. (He may not be able to afford champagne and lobster). This will give you a clear view of what's in his budget. If he suggests an inexpensive wine by the glass, accompanied by a pasta dish, order accordingly.

When the check comes, reach for your purse and watch his reaction. If he doesn't stop you, go one step further and offer to contribute. Most gentlemen will appreciate the gesture, but refuse your money. Thank him for the good company and the enjoyable conversation but remember, you don't owe him anything more, even if he did pay for the meal. He, too, had a wonderful evening.

CLOSING THE DEAL

All good things must come to an end. I know you want it to go on forever, but you must keep him yearning for more—for another date.

Dear Jula,
I forgot my date's name and he won't let me hear the end of it. I'd like to keep seeing him, but he's driving me crazy by repeatedly saying, "My name is John, in case you forget." I wish he'd just let it go. How can I make him stop?

Mary Jane

When the inevitable moment is upon you, say something like, "Tonight has been incredible. It's really been a pleasure." This statement strokes his ego while letting him know, in not so many words, that you're ready to call it a night. He'll offer to take you home and ask to see you again.

Not all dates are good; some should end before they even begin. It's perfectly acceptable to end a date whenever you see fit, just end it politely. If your eyes are rolling in the back of your head and you have a bad case of the yawns, it's time to go. Excuse yourself and go to the ladies room. When you return, kindly say, "I'm not feeling well. I need to go home. I hate to disrupt your dinner so I'll just catch a cab."

Dear Mary Jane,
He's making a big deal out of some-thing he should've just laughed off. Tell him once more that you're sorry and ask him to drop it. If he doesn't, stop dating him and let him know why: "You see John, it's like this John. You're driving me insane and turn-ing me off John. Goodbye John."

Jula Jane

Notice how you didn't apologize (this will make him think he has another chance), and you didn't offer to go out some other time. You merely stated that you weren't feeling well and that you were going to go home. In plain English: "I'm not enjoying your company and I don't want to see you again." Quick and painless.

THE NEXT LEVEL

We've covered the basics, now it's time to go deeper and be-come more technical. To master the art of dating, you must understand what motivates you and what motivates him.

DESPERATELY
SEEKING VALIDATION

I am sad to say that very few women ever experience the un-conditional love of a father they so desperately need. Unfortunately, this void affects a woman's soul very deeply and impacts how she relates to men in her personal life. This is why so many women do just about anything to attract male attention. I can't fix the problem—it's deep-rooted and requires therapy—but I sure can ease the pain.

Wouldn't it be wonderful to hear, "I love you, baby girl, no matter what." What a validation it is to know that you're worthy of love simply for who you are. The only way you're ever going to hear these sweet, sweet words is to hold out for a man who will not only say them to you, but also mean what he's saying. He's out there; we just have to get you up to speed so you can find him.

GAME ON

Let's face it, girls. We know what we want from a man, and we know what a man wants from us. The trick is getting what we want while leading him to think he's in control and getting what *he* wants. Ultimately, a woman seeks security and love, which usually translates into marriage. A man wants sex—pure and simple.

Scene 1: Man meets woman. Man buys woman drink. Man says nice things to her. She tries on his last name. Thinks it's perfect. Man buys woman another drink. Thinks he's gonna score! Man tells woman she's the prettiest girl in the bar. She believes him and beams. Man asks woman to go to his place to give him decorating ideas. She thinks he wants her to move in.

Scene 2: Man takes woman to his place, lights candles and gives her a glass of wine. She thinks he's so romantic. He thinks he's smooth and is gonna score. Man gives woman the tour of

Dear Jula,
I'm sleeping with an 18-year-old guy and think I'm falling in love with him. He's fun, makes me laugh, and he's great in bed. Does it matter that he's starting college in the fall and I'm a 35-year-old married woman with children? Did I mention he's my girlfriend's son and she caught me going down on him at her beach house and has forbidden us to see each other? Details.
Mrs. Robinson

Dear Mrs. Robinson, I don't even know where to begin. Yes, it's wrong. He's too young for you, you're married, and he's your friend's son. If you were single and he wasn't heir to a friend, it would be a lot easier for me to say, "What the hell, you're just dating for fun. Knock yourself out." But that's not the case. You need to end this affair immediately. Period.
Jula Jane

his bachelor pad, explaining it just needs a woman's touch. She hears, "I want to marry you." He's thinking, "I'm gonna score!" Man shows woman his bedroom and kisses her. She melts. He scores! Man takes woman back to her car and says, "I'll call you tomorrow." Woman goes home and plans the wedding. Man never calls woman. Woman wonders why.

Hello, Ladies! Are you nuts? Why should he call? A man likes to hunt, to chase. He wants to feel like something is out of his reach, not easily attained. If given a chance, he will pursue you. Give him the chance. So you're thinking, "I shouldn't have to play games. If a man truly loves me it will happen naturally." If that's your philosophy on dating, let me ask you one question: How's that working for you?

I'm not a fan of playing games, either, but I do believe in male-female roles and setting the stage for romance to unfold. If you set your standards high and don't settle for less, a man who is genuinely interested will live up to those standards, for fear of losing you if he doesn't.

THE THRILL OF THE HUNT

Picture a man on a deer hunt. He wears camouflage pants and a jacket, carries his favorite gun and has a plan of action. He ventures into the woods in search of a 10-point buck. The thrill of the hunt excites him, gets his blood flowing.

He steps five feet into the woods and is confronted by a deer. At first he's excited; his adrenaline pumps as he prepares for the chase. He raises his shotgun but before he can shoot, the deer falls to the ground. "Take me, I'm yours." The man begrudgingly shoots his prey and throws it into the back of his truck and goes home feeling disappointed.

The deer threw himself at the hunter in the way we throw ourselves at any man who pays attention to us. Boring!! Had the deer valued itself more, it would have turned and run, letting only the best man win him in the hunt of a lifetime. There are many hunters out there willing to pursue you. Run and don't look back. When the best man captures your heart, you both win.

CHIVALRY LIVES!

If you want the man in your life to treat you like a lady and open your door, guide him. When he forgets, quietly let him remember simply by staying in the car or standing in front of a door but not opening it. He'll get the hint and appreciate that you didn't bring attention to his error. If you want him to stand when you leave the table (this is slightly old school), then linger by your chair until he rises. A true gentleman will understand what you're doing and in the future, he'll oblige voluntarily. If you prefer he take charge, stand back and let him lead the way. When you walk into a restaurant, don't storm the hostess stand. Walk by his side and allow him to announce your arrival. This slight gesture says, "I trust you." Men love that.

Chivalry isn't dead—as long as we don't kill it. Frankly, we've confused men. Some of us want them to open our door while others snap, "I can do it myself." You can still be a feminist, even if you let a man open your door. He's not implying you can't do it yourself, he's merely showing respect. Embrace a man's kind gestures and enjoy being a woman. There's no shame in that.

Many women pursue men, believing they shouldn't have to wait for a man to call or initiate dates. It's the 21st century, for God's sake! A woman should be able to call a man and ask him out! *Really?*

This is merely an excuse for those not patient enough to wait. Go ahead and ask a guy out to dinner. Go one step further and pay the tab. You've just accomplished nothing. He may go, but I guarantee he won't pursue you from that moment on. He may not even grant you a second date—unless he's looking for a free meal. Picture the deer chasing the hunter. What's the hunter going to do? RUN! That's what.

THE CALLING GAME

The calling game is the most nerve-racking thing in the dating world. Should you call him or wait for him to call you? And if he never calls, is it then okay to call him? Your mind wanders: Maybe he lost my number, maybe he called but I never got the message, maybe I'm making up any excuse I can think of so I can justify calling him.

Let's break this down and make it simple. DO NOT UNDER ANY CIRCUMSTANCE CALL HIM FIRST! When you meet a man you're interested in and he asks for your number, give it to him and wait patiently for him to call. I don't care if a month goes by. Do not Google him to get his number and call him. I mean it, DON'T DO IT!

A guy struggles with the opposite dilemma. Should he call

immediately, or wait a few days? If he calls too soon he appears desperate. But if he waits too long, he may piss her off. Most guys wait two to three days. After that you can safely assume he's not as into you as he led you to believe.

POWER BALL

Once the calls have begun we must still follow the same simple rule—do not call him first! I can't stress this enough. When we call a man, we are pursuing him. This is a case of the duck using the duck call instead of the hunter. It just doesn't make sense.

You may hear guys claim they like it when a woman calls them. They're either lying or they are delusional. They don't like it. Let him call you and either answer his call, or let it go to voicemail and return it within 24 hours. The exception to this rule is if he's the type that leaves you hanging for days on end. If that's the case, return the favor.

This is where the real game playing begins. I call it Power Ball. When a guy leaves you a voicemail, he essentially tosses you the Power Ball. You now have the option to call him back or not, knowing his ego hangs in the balance. If you call him back immediately, you seem desperate or too into him. If you wait a day or two, he may become intrigued, if not a little smitten with you. Wait too long and he will get mad because you hurt his pride. But he will still be interested.

This is not an exact science and should be altered for your individual situation. Keep in mind that the minute you return his call, you are tossing the Power Ball back to him and must now wait for him to respond. Monitor your emotions and thoughts while you wait for him to call you back and you will get a glimpse of what he's feeling when the roles are reversed. Empowering, isn't it?

CAN'T BUY ME LOVE

I will say this once, girls. Don't buy gifts for men. It will seem as though you're trying to buy his affection, which will turn him off. Trust me on this one. I can't tell you how many men have told me stories of women showering them with cute cards, flowers, and presents. Not one of them liked it. In fact, it made them feel obligated to return the favor, and feeling obligated to do something is the kiss of death for men.

It's never a good idea to buy a gift for a man you're casually dating. Wait until you're in a relationship and even then, limit the gift-giving to his birthday and Christmas. Just because you like giving, it doesn't mean he likes receiving. Recall the *Sex and the City* episode where Charlotte bought her new man expen- sive briefs. He felt she was moving too fast and quit dating her. It happens all the time. And making gifts for him isn't al- lowed, either. That includes compiling your favorite love songs onto a CD, mak- ing a scrapbook with photos and movie stubs from your dates, and crafting homemade cards. It's not sexy and it's not enticing; it's a turn-off.

MAID OR MISTRESS

Stop folding the laundry; leave the dirty dishes in the sink; and back away from the vacuum. A man doesn't want you to tidy up after him; he wants you to seduce him! I know you want to show him you'd make a great wife, but he's more interested in your talents between the sheets than in how adept you are at washing the sheets. He wants a sex goddess around the house, not a maid.

Remember, you're not his girlfriend and you're not his wife, nor are you his maid. You're simply a fabulous girl he's dating. It's not your job to clean his place, no matter how filthy it is. If it's too much to bear, suggest spending more time at your house. Enough said.

PLAYING HOUSE

When you are having an intimate relationship with a man, you visit his home, frequently sleep over, and essentially play house. You leave personal belongings for "convenience"—a toothbrush, maybe some feminine products, extra panties, your favorite CD. In time, you leave even more items, like pajamas, work clothes, a hair dryer, makeup, etc. and before you know it, half your wardrobe is at his place. This will cause him to feel suffocated and you, to become attached.

Instead of slowly moving in with him (without him asking you to), I recommend you put together an overnight bag with your essential items and take it to and from his place. Never leave it there. This shows respect for his space and keeps you liberated.

He'll see that you aren't completely whipped and that you have a life outside of him. For all he knows, this overnight bag may travel with you to places other than just his home. I know this may sound manipulative, but believe me, it works. Before long, he will yearn to have you all to himself and move towards a stronger commitment—living together and/or marriage.

This goes both ways. Don't allow him to leave his things at your place, either. This will make him wonder why, plus he will feel a little shunned. This is good for a man. If you encourage him to set up house in your place, again, he'll feel suffocated and back away. The other reason for all of this is to create a feeling of inconvenience for him. If he has to put forth effort every time he wants to see you, he'll naturally move towards a commitment more quickly to make his life easier. Remember, you have a home. Don't invade his.

THAT FOUR-LETTER WORD

Such a sweet sentiment can be the kiss of death. Never tell a man you love him first. Don't do it. Let him be in control of this statement. Wait for a man to say, "I love you" first, and he'll feel like he's chasing you, trying to make you love him back.

And when he does finally say those three magical words, don't feel like you need to say them back right away. Wait until you truly mean it. The best response when you're not ready to say "I love you" is: "I love the way that sounds. Say it again." You're sparing his feelings at a very vulnerable moment and setting the stage for the time when you do share those same feelings.

How many of you have told a man you love him within a few days of dating? You know who you are. Why did you do it and what was the reaction? Every time a man has done this to me, I run. I know there's no way he can be in love with me so soon, so I take it as a line. Keep those precious words to yourself as long as you possibly can. The end result will be a lot more effective.

THE BUSY SIGNAL

Which has more perceived value—an object that's hard to acquire or one that's easy to get? Something becomes a collector's item for one main reason—it has limited availability. Let me rephrase that: he pays more for diamonds than he does for sapphires because diamonds are more precious. I'm not comparing you to objects with price tags; I'm merely demonstrating how you can become more sought after by men—by being less available.

If a man can reach you every time he tries to call you, he'll perceive you as easy to get. If you're not available, sometimes for days, he'll perceive you as hard to get. Mr. Big on *Sex & the City* was dating a famous actress who would rarely take his calls. It drove him wild and made him like her even more. This method works like a charm in real life, too.

Keep him guessing by turning him down every so often without giving a reason. Simply thank him for the invitation and let him know you can't make it. Women tend to give too many details and not allow a man's imagination to run wild. Let him wonder who's taking precedence over him.

Make damn sure you aren't an after-thought or a last-minute replacement for someone else; never accept a date on the same day it's asked. If he doesn't value you enough to plan ahead, he isn't worth your time. There's an exception to this rule: the hugely successful man who travels a lot for work. You need to be flex-ible with your time if you want to date this type of man. If he takes advantage of your flexibility, stop dating him and tell him why.

You should never, ever blow off plans with your girlfriends to accommodate a man. This will show him that he takes prec-edence over everyone else, empowering him a little too much. I can assure you; he won't put you ahead of his friends. Just say no on occasion and never worry about him losing interest because of it. He won't.

WHY BUY THE COW WHEN YOU CAN GET THE MILK FOR FREE?

A woman dates a man with the hope of becoming his girlfriend. I think that's a grave mistake. When you become a man's "girlfriend" you give him control over you without even realizing it. You become completely devoted to him, as you forsake all other suitors, and basically, pretend to be his wife. When he has you all to himself (and he knows it), he's less likely to commit fully to marriage.

As a single and fabulous woman, you should feel entitled to date whomever you choose, and do whatever you please, without answering to anyone. And unless you're sporting a man's last name, you're free to "try on"–this is a term I've grown to love—as many different men as you see fit.

Relationships are for people who are
waiting for something better to come along.
—Sara, gossip columnist in Hitch

The idea of an exclusive relationship without an engagement or marriage or at least a monogamy ring is absurd to me. You have your house, I have mine, and we'll agree to not see anyone else. We spend every night at each other's house, with the exception of guys' and girls' night out. We take years to decide if the other is good enough for us and eventually, we break up or cheat on each other. I believe you know right away if you want to marry someone. If not, enjoy it but don't commit, or worse, pretend to.

Dating is different from a relationship and it's different from an engagement, and it's different from a marriage, so don't treat it like it's something it's not. Dating is a time to get to know one another. Be smart, be aware, and be crazy—that's what being single and dating is all about. Don't get bogged down with the details, just enjoy the moment.

Are You a Great Date or a One-Date Wonder?

1. When your date asks you to meet him at a restaurant at 7:30 you:
   A. Show up thirty minutes early to ensure you won't be late.
   B. Arrive at precisely 7:30—showing respect for yourself as well as for your date.
   C. Get there an hour late to prove you're worth waiting for.

2. On a first date, you talk about:
   A. Yourself and all the things you like to do—shopping, getting manicures, hanging out with girlfriends and going to chick flicks.
   B. Your ex-boyfriends, to try and make him jealous.
   C. Interesting things like vacation hot spots, food and wine, and current events.

3. Your idea of a great outfit is:
   A. Something elegant yet flirty, not too skimpy but not frumpy either—in other words, something you look and feel great in.
   B. Anything that shows a lot of cleavage or leg—or both.
   C. Sweats and tennis shoes—he should like you no matter what you wear.

4. Dating to you is:
   A. A necessary evil if you want to land a husband.
   B. A constant adventure, a fun and exhilarating thrill ride.
   C. A grueling experience that you avoid at all costs.

5. After three dates with the same man you:
    A. Consider yourself his girlfriend and wonder where it's going.
    B. Look forward to the fourth date and don't give the future much thought.
    C. Tell him you love him.

6. When ordering dinner you:
    A. Let your date know what you'd like and let him order for you.
    B. Take forever to make up your mind and finally choose the house salad—no egg, extra peppers (green, not red), carrots, cucumbers, and scallions, oh, and tomatoes—the cherry kind, not sliced. You make the waiter run down the entire list of dressings and always go with your favorite—blue cheese.
    C. Mispronounce entrees and butcher the wine list: "I'd like the soup dooger and some of them there ham crockets and uh, a glass of peanut greejo."

7. When the check comes you:
    A. Hand it to him and expect him to pay.
    B. Retreat to the ladies' room hoping he'll pick up the tab.
    C. Reach for your wallet. If he offers to pay, you kindly accept and thank him. If he says nothing, you offer to contribute and lay down enough cash to cover your meal.

8. If a guy offers to take you to a sporting event you:
    A. Accept his invitation, whether you like sports or not—you're in it for the pleasure of his company not the venue.
    B. Roll your eyes and tell him you hate sports and that you would rather watch paint dry.
    C. Decide to go, but complain the entire time and send him for refreshments just as the bases are loaded and his favorite player is on deck.

9. A perfect date to you is:

A. Getting flown to an exotic locale and being spoiled with shopping, champagne and spa treatments.

B. When he actually shows up.

C. Spending time with someone you find interesting and fun—no matter where you go or what you do.

10. At the end of a date you:

A. Smother him with kisses and practically beg him to spend the night.

B. Give him a hug and maybe a kiss, and tell him that you had a wonderful time.

C. Ask if he'd like to see you again—and when.

Quiz Results

You're a great date if you chose the following answers:

1. **B.** You show consideration for other people and for yourself, which is a very attractive quality.

2. **C.** Keeping the conversation light and fun will ensure your dates come back for more.

3. **A.** Taking pride in your appearance and always being appropriate is a surefire way to attract men. They'll be drawn to you, not just your cleavage.

4. **B.** You enjoy dating for what it is—a chance to get to know new people and experience new things. Your cup is half full.

5. **B.** You're in no rush to settle down or, more specifically—to settle, so you enjoy each date to the fullest with no expectations. This will lead to fewer disappointments and mismatches.

6. **A.** You enjoy letting a man care for you, which shows you're confident enough to rely on others. He'll love you for it.

7. **C.** You appreciate when a man picks up the tab, but you don't expect it—that goes a long way.

8. **A.** You're a fun person who makes the most out of any given situation. You go with the flow and aren't too uptight. Men love women like that.

9. **C.** Lavish dates are fun but they're not essential for you to have a good time. Getting to know someone new is what you enjoy the most, and it shows.

10. **B.** You are a woman who knows the value of keeping a little mystery about her. Because you don't give too much too soon, you keep him guessing so he's intrigued.

chapter 5

Flirt Boot Camp

Secret #5:
The Power to Control Your Dating Destiny Is in You

Sex appeal is fifty percent what you've got and
fifty percent what people think you've got.
—Sophia Loren

You've heard of military boot camp and you've heard of fitness boot camp. I bring you Flirt Boot Camp. Flirt Boot Camp consists of five days of intense training and intense flirting. You'll learn how to take a man's breath away with a glance, and how to control an entire room with your smile. It's going to be fun, it's going to be hard, and it's going to be effective. Read through this chapter completely and then dedicate a week to putting it into action. Now, start flirting!

DAY 1
A HEALTHY ROUTINE

MORNING

Step 1: Get up one hour earlier than normal. Brush your teeth, comb your hair, throw on your favorite work-out outfit, and do something active for 30 minutes. If you belong to a gym, go. And if you don't, head outside and walk or run a few miles. If it's raining cats and dogs, stay in and stay active. Do sit-ups, push-ups and lunges for 30 minutes.

Step 2: Take a shower and shave your legs. Put on your makeup, style your hair, and dress up in something that makes you feel put together, such as a suit for work, or trendy jeans and a sweater for play. Make sure your clothes match and don't have wrinkles or holes. You'd think most people would know this, but I've learned from experience that this is not necessarily so.

Step 3: Scramble a couple of eggs, skip the toast and juice (too much sugar!) and put on a pot of coffee, preferably decaf. Water is even better. While you enjoy your breakfast, read at least one article about world affairs—and I don't mean a tabloid story about Lindsay Lohan's latest D.U.I.

Seductive Stare
Step 4: Now that you're looking great, feeling energized, and are slightly more informed, I want you to stand in front of a mirror and flirt with yourself. You may feel silly at first, but do it anyway. Make sure you're alone. After all, if you're too shy to flirt with yourself, how will you ever be able to flirt with a handsome man?

First, pretend you see a hot guy across a crowded room. Look at "him" in the mirror. Gesture how you normally would. If you just winked and licked your lips, I want you to promise never to do that again. I mean it, *never*. Now, try something different.

Make eye contact with him, holding your gaze a second past comfortable. Smile sweetly and slowly turn away, almost resting your chin on your shoulder, then slowly turn back towards him with a confident grin, eyes gazing into his. You just said, "Hello, I find you attractive." Now turn away from him and pay attention to your friends. The ball is in his court. If you performed the seductive stare ritual correctly, he'll be by your side in a matter of minutes. And if not, try, try again.

Practice your gaze over and over until it feels natural. There are to be no awkward moments in your future. Good, now it's time to go to work, or where ever you go on a daily basis. But bring your book with you. You're free until lunch, but afterwards, you're mine. Go by yourself to a nice café or restaurant with a happening scene, and order a light lunch, such as fish or chicken with veggies, and a bottle of water. Then open your book to this page. No peeking until then.

NOON
ACTION / REACTION
It's hard to dine alone, but it's important that you do. I want you out of the house as often as possible, and you're more approachable when you're alone. Think about it from his perspective. It's hard enough for a man to approach a woman, but when she has someone next to her, it's even harder.

Now it's time to practice what I preach. I want you to scan the room in search of a handsome man. Make sure he's by himself; he's more likely to approach you. Make eye contact and give him your sweet smile and shy retreat, followed by your confident gaze. Don't be shy. You practiced this all morning. Now you're ready. Turn your attention away from him and back to your book.

Your number one goal is not to meet men, at least, not today. Your number one goal is to boost your confidence and perfect your flirt. Don't get discouraged if your target doesn't come over. It's lunchtime and he has a busy day ahead of him, though he would love to meet you. It's just that he knows he doesn't have enough time to sweep you off your feet. The point is, don't get discouraged. Practice makes perfect.

I want you to flirt with five different men before you leave the restaurant. I don't care if you have to flirt with the bus boy, just keep flirting. And to keep you on track, you have to write a description of all five lucky men whose day you made by making them feel attractive. Read the Flirts example and then give it a try.

FLIRTS: (EXAMPLE)

1. Hot guy sitting at the bar eating a burger and chatting with the bartender. He smiled back, but didn't come over. He must be gay.

2. Average man in a business suit just finishing his meal. He came over, introduced himself, said he had to get back to work but really wanted to get to know me. He asked for my number and said he'd call. I believe him.

3. Sexy bartender. He sent me a free drink, a Sex on the Beach. I wonder what he's implying.

4. Waiter. The crowd has thinned and it's slim pickings. We flirted until he brought my check. No discount, no number. Next.

5. Handsome man waiting for his lunch companion to come out of the men's room. My mesmerizing flirt must have worked because he blew off his friend and joined me at my table. We were both finished with lunch but made time for a cup of coffee and flirtatious banter. We exchanged numbers and set a date for Friday night. Score!

Not bad for your first try. Now go back to work or wherever you need to go and take a break from all this flirting. You earned it. One more thing before you go: Call your best friend and invite her to happy hour tonight at your favorite place. Be sure to bring your book. You're going to need it.

NIGHT
Wing Woman

Make your way to the bar and flirt your way into a good spot, somewhere with a view of the entire place. Order a glass of red wine for you and your partner in crime and clue her in on what you're doing—Flirt Boot Camp.

Show her your results from lunch and invite her to go through Flirt Boot Camp with you. It's so much more fun training with someone than doing it all on your own. You can keep each other motivated and become each other's wing woman. You'll probably be approached by men wondering what you're reading. Tell them you've enrolled in Flirt Boot Camp and watch the smiles come across their faces.

Periodically, send your girlfriend to the ladies' room so you can practice your flirt on unsuspecting men without distraction. When she comes out, it's her job to become incognito and watch your actions, and those of the men, too. Then she must report back to you. You can take turns doing this.

Keep this up as long as you can. Hopefully, you'll have so much fun, you won't want to stop. Flirt all night long, if you like. This is what Day 1 is all about—practicing your new flirting technique. When you get home, record your results. This time I want you to analyze your own actions and that of the men so you can learn from them.

DAY 2
TURNING HEADS

MORNING

Repeat steps 1–3 (Exercise, get dressed and get fueled.) You can eat something different if you like, but keep it healthy and low-cal.

Step 4: Now, it's time for technique. It's important to make an unforgettable entrance so that everyone in the room wants to meet you. It's a lot easier than it sounds, so don't be nervous. I'm going to guide you step-by-seductive step, then we'll practice. Go ahead and read through the next few paragraphs.

The dance begins at the door. When you walk into a room, hesitate in the doorway for just a moment. (If you're with friends, let them go ahead. You'll join them soon enough.) Scan the room confidently, as if you're looking for someone. Be cognizant of your posture. Your head should be held high, your shoulders back, and your arms hanging comfortably by your sides. You must come off as confident and controlled, never nervous or fidgety.

Make eye contact with a friendly face in the center of the room, and walk in his direction. You want to show everyone who you are and what you're made of—confidence. Glide through the crowd, politely making eye contact with several people, both men and women, along the way. When you get to the center of the room, pause a few seconds then scan the crowd for your friends. Smile at them and slowly make your way to the safety of their company. Remember to breathe.

Now that everyone knows you're there, make them come to you. Show how approachable you are: Laugh with your friends, treat the wait staff with respect, make eye contact with everyone you're speaking to, and keep your body language open by facing the crowd with your arms uncrossed and your purse down by your side. You're there to make new acquaintances, not to hide.

Let's practice. Go to the main entrance of your home and do exactly what you just read. Pause, make eye contact, and play a game. You can't touch me and I can't touch you until we get home. Then we can devour each other as we wish. I think the anticipation will drive us wild."

This way you're not hurting his feelings by telling him he's doing something wrong. You're merely suggesting a fun way to turn each other on. Reward him when you get home and continue this "game" until it becomes a habit. Your days of PDAs will be over before you know it.

Jula Jane

proceed. Pretend your living room is a crowded bar and make your way through the hordes of people. Scan the vast room for your friends. There they are, now go to them. Carry on a mock conversation and critique yourself. Are you open and approachable? Is your head held high, and are your shoulders pulled back?

Pep Talk

Did you feel silly? Good. Do it again and keep doing it until you don't feel silly. I want you to own this. Some of you may be thinking this isn't possible for you to pull off. You feel you're not pretty enough, or thin enough, or secure enough to domi-nate a room. But before you count your-self out, let me be clear about something. Any woman can be the center of atten-tion and any woman—short, fat, tall, or skinny—has it in her to turn heads. You just have to know what you're doing and act confidently while doing it.

Good work. That's enough for now. Check back in at lunch. You can go to a restaurant or eat at your desk—you're going to be reading for a little while.

NOON

Revelations

Welcome back. I hope you're enjoying your lunch. Now, I'm going to explain what we're doing. I know my methods may seem a bit unorthodox, so I appreciate you following them nonetheless.

Flirting is one of the key elements in dating, and to be a good flirt, you have to be confident. I'm trying to build your confidence one step at a time with tips that may seem unre-lated, but are necessary. You may be wondering, "What does getting up early, exercising, eating healthy, and reading the newspaper have to do with flirting?" The answer is *everything!*

I'm making you get up one hour early each day so you have time to practice these techniques. I want you to exercise and eat healthy, not only to help you lose weight, but also to help boost your energy level and to help you get into the rhythm of developing positive habits. As for reading the paper, this will come in handy when your new flirt technique lands you a man and you need to sound intelligent while making conversation. Study the day's headlines each and every day and you will always have something interesting to talk about. Make all of these habits part of your lifestyle and your confidence will begin to grow—and it will continue to grow as you keep nourishing them. See, there really is a method to my madness!

Here's why I'm making you practice flirt techniques at home. It's really quite simple: You're more likely to flirt in public if you've mastered flirting at home.

Practical Lessons

Imagine yourself back in the doorway of club elite. You look spectacular—you're wearing a stunning outfit, your head is held high, and your confidence is palpable. Now, pause. Let them take you in, and just as you're about to enter the room, give your famous flirtatious glance to a handsome stranger in the center of the room. In the first lesson you only made eye contact with him; this time you're giving him "the look." Every man will wish he was the object of your affection.

Slowly and gracefully make your way through the bar gracing one, maybe two, lucky men with your infectious gaze. As you finally reach center stage, make an abrupt turn and but don't over-inflate his ego. "My heart stops when I look in to your eyes." Yuck.

Ask him specific questions about his day rather than just asking how his day was. It goes something like this: "How did your meeting go with KBR?" This shows you're interested in him and his work, and that you listen when he speaks. Remove "How was your day," from your vocabulary. It's too common and will fall on deaf ears. Continue feeding his ego in this specific fashion and he'll know where your heart is.

Jula Jane

head to the bar, as if you suddenly remembered something. This seductive dance will captivate everyone around you. Men will want you and women will envy you—if you do it well. And that's why you practice at home.

Another Pep Talk

I sense fear and hesitation from some of you, and I think I know why. You still feel like you can't pull this off. You think that only drop-dead gorgeous women, not an average woman like yourself, can garner this kind of attention. The truth is, average women probably receive *more* attention. It's true. Men tend to feel more comfortable approaching women who aren't overly-attractive because average women are viewed as non-threatening and less likely to reject them.

Beauty is definitely in the eye of the beholder. Not all men want a Pamela Anderson or a Heidi Klum. A lot of men prefer a Rachel Ray or a Queen Latifah. Embrace your body type and your one-of-a-kind look and others will embrace it, too. Apologize for it and they will assume something's wrong. So the next time you don't feel pretty enough, scan the room and notice how all the 10's are standing alone while all the 5's, 6's, 7's and 8's are landing dates.

It's not only important to accept yourself, it's equally important to accept compliments. Have you ever noticed how some women reject flattering words? Instead of graciously accepting a compliment, they discard them. Learn from their mistakes. The next time someone says, "Wow, you have an incredible smile," respond with, "Thank you. That's sweet of you to say." And smile.

Dear Jula,
I'm a woman on a mission and I need to learn a new trick. Please tell me the most effective way to flirt.

Juliana

Dear Juliana,
The single most effective flirting technique is to mirror a man's body language. It's simple and will yield immediate results. Match his movements. Whatever he does, you do. Don't be awkward about it, though. Keep it natural. If he leans in on his elbows, then lean in on your elbows. If he crosses his legs, cross yours.

You don't want him to think you're making fun of him by imitating his every move so wait between five and 60 seconds to follow his lead. This way he won't realize what you're doing. He'll just know he likes it.

Jula Jane

You are to spend the rest of your lunch hour practicing putting your flirtatious stare together with your dramatic entrance. Play it out in your head over and over until you feel comfortable with it, and then get back to work. But first, I need to tell you what's on tonight's agenda: You're going to go out by yourself and try this out in public. You don't have to stay long, just long enough to make an entrance and reap the rewards, approximately 30 minutes. You can give this book a rest for now, but remember to take it with you this evening.

NIGHT
The Inside Scoop

This takes guts and I know you have what it takes. Let's do this right. Repeat steps 1–3: exercise, eat something healthy, read the paper, shower and make yourself dazzling. Unless you're going to happy hour straight from work, never go out with the morning's makeup on. A fresh face will make you feel and look better, as will a change of clothes. Practice your look and your entrance five more times. Now, go!

Choose a bar or restaurant where you know the staff. It's safer and you'll have someone familiar to talk to. On that note, here's a tip. Make the bartender your new best friend. Once he bonds with you, he'll always make sure you get a good seat. He'll serve you first, he'll keep you company when you're flying solo, and best of all, he'll introduce you to great men and steer you clear of jerks. In return, always tip well. If he comps your drinks, tip according to what your bill would have been, plus a little extra.

This goes back to thinking and acting like a man. Because they're accustomed to paying the tab, men know that in order to get good service, you have to pay extra for it. For example, when you pull up to the valet, tip him 20 bucks and ask him to keep your car close by. He'll probably park it right up front. This is a great way to stand out in a crowd. People notice when some-one receives preferential treatment, so use that to your advantage. Just like men do.

Now make your entrance . . .

Bravo, you did it! Retreat to the bar, order a bottle of water and wait ten minutes before ordering a glass of wine. You're giving all the men a chance to work up the nerve to approach you, and offering to buy you a drink is an easy opener for them. You don't want to take that away from them by already having ordered a drink yourself. If you're feeling a bit overwhelmed, let the bartender know you'll be right back and escape to the ladies' room. Regroup and enter with style and confidence. You'll probably get stopped on your way back to the bar, and you may even be followed. I'm a huge fan of the bathroom retreat. It gets you in the mix and makes you approachable.

If the night's going well, stay as long as you're comfortable. Have fun and flirt, but go home alone. If you're not having

IS HE
INTERESTED?

Dear Jula,
How can I tell if a man is interested in me or not?
Penny

Dear Penny,
The first sign of a man's interest can be seen on his face. His eyebrows will raise, his lips will part, and his nostrils will flare, ever so slightly, only for a split second. He's saying, "I like what I see."

The next move he makes will be designed to get your attention. He'll stand away from the crowd, allowing you to get a good look at him, and he'll start to fidget. Watch for him to run his hands through his hair or adjust his tie; he's subconsciously trying to look good for you.

These may seem like common gestures, but they're so much more. His body language speaks louder than his words ever will. Watch him closely and you'll see what I mean.
Jula Jane

much luck, pay for your drink, thank the bartender, and call it a night. No matter what happens, the night was a success. You just passed Day 2 of Flirt Boot Camp. Get some sleep.

DAY 3
CHARMER

You know the drill. Repeat steps 1–3. This won't change. It's going to be the same on Day 4 and on Day 5. I swear it's for your own good.

Step 4: Today you're going to flirt with everyone and everything. Say hello to the concierge in your building. Better yet, stop for a minute and let him know how much you appreciate him. When you walk into your office, smile at the lobby receptionist and tell her she looks great today. Ask her if she's lost weight. Answer your phone with a sweet smile and a sunny disposition. Invite a co-worker to lunch. Tip the waiter a little extra and tell him what a great job he's doing. Call your best friend and let her know how special she is to you. And when you get home, give your dog a lot of attention. Pet his belly, kiss his face, and tell him you love him.

I want you to absolutely charm the pants off everyone you come in contact with today. This is going to become part of your everyday lifestyle, even on PMS days, so embrace it. Make a conscious effort to do this every day and before you know it, it will become second nature. The fact is, flirting makes you feel good about yourself and it makes others feel good about themselves. And as an added bonus, it makes you look amazing in the eyes of a man. People naturally flock towards happy people and when you flirt, you appear to be happy. The next time you're out on a date and see a pretty girl walk by, say, "Wow, she's gorgeous." Your date won't be enthralled by her; he'll be enthralled by you, a woman so confident in herself that she can appreciate other women.

DAY 4
TALK TO STRANGERS

MORNING
Repeat steps 1 -3 with a smile.

Step 4: Did your mother tell you, "Never talk to strangers?" That's great advice for a little girl, but it's not so great for a single woman. You have to talk to strangers and sometimes you have to initiate the conversation, if you want to meet new people.

When you see a man you'd like to meet, casually go stand next to him. Don't crowd him, but do stand close enough to invite conversation. Try to make eye contact for a second or two, give a nice bright smile, and then look away. If he responds in kind, he's open to chatting, but if he looks away or gives you a close-mouthed smile, move on. He's probably not interested.

Opening Lines
"Hey baby, do you come here often?" We've all heard this cheesy line before. Does it work? No, not usually. Canned pick-up lines aren't effective so try something natural. "Have you eaten here before? I'm torn between the pastrami and the chicken salad. What do you think?" Keep your opening lines appropriate to the situation you're in; the more ordinary, the better: "Is there really a difference between regular, unleaded and premium gas?" These are

---

LAW OF SCARCITY

Dear Jula,
How do I make a guy fall for me in the beginning? Do I play hard to get or do I jockey for as much face time as possible?
Pamela

Dear Pamela,
You must win his heart, or at least his mind, before you employ the hard-to-get strategy. It's proven that re-peated exposure to almost any stimulus will make you like it more. This holds true for men *and* women. The more he's around you; the more he'll like you.
When you have him under your spell, pull back. Become less and less available until you hardly see him at all. This will instigate the law of scarcity. He'll want what he can't have. Continue this "game" for as long as you deem appropriate, then slowly ease him back into your life. He'll be in love and ready to commit by the time you do.
Jula Jane

non-threatening ways to start a conversation with a handsome stranger. You just opened the door for him to pursue you without the pressure of rejection hanging over his head. *Hello*, stranger!

Armchair seduction

Find your favorite chair in your house. Now approach it like you would a good-looking man. Casually walk over to it and scan the room, as if you're looking for someone. Turn towards the chair and make eye contact for a second or two, then smile and look away. That wasn't so hard, was it? Now start up a conversation: "I hear the sushi here is incredible. Have you tried it?" If he wants to chat with you, he'll smile, move in closer to you, and continue the conversation. I know your chair isn't going to make a move on you, but pretend it has and keep the banter going.

Try to ask questions that demand an intelligent, thoughtful answer. Stay away from yes or no questions. "What do you like about this place?" works; "Do you come here often?" does not. You want to draw him out and keep him talking for as long as possible. The longer you're together, the more comfortable you'll both become. Pay attention to his body language, though. If he starts to look away, that means he's bored and looking for his escape. Give it to him or change the subject to something more interesting. Refer back to your morning headlines and wow him with your knowledge.

Approach your chair as many times as you can before work, trying different openers each time. Good work. See you at lunch.

NOON AND NIGHT
Hello, My Name Is . . .

Before you go home, I want you to meet five new men. This may take you hours and require you to go to several different places, but it's worth it. Use the techniques and opening lines we discussed this morning, and by the end of the day, you'll have at least one date lined up for the weekend.

Remember: Approach anyone you find attractive by asking the simple question, "Pardon me, do you have the time?" That's it for today. Happy hunting!

DAY 5
GIRLS' DAY

MORNING

Call all of your favorite, single girlfriends (leave the catty ones at home!) and invite them to your house for some undisclosed fun. Tell them to bring their gym clothes, toiletries, a casual outfit, and some flirty evening attire. Prepare a delicious breakfast for everyone—lots of fruit, hard-boiled eggs, cheese and crackers, and because you've worked so hard this week, champagne. Make mimosas or frozen Bellinis. Yummy!

Gather everyone in the living room. As you serve your scrumptious breakfast, clue them in on the day's activities. (You may read from the book if you need to.)

Here's a brief rundown of the day's agenda:

➣ Eat, gossip, and drink champagne.

➣ Fill out "Great Man" profiles (as in Chapter 1) and share answers.

➣ Create a "Wing Woman" plan of action.

➣ Workout. Flirt.

➣ Shower and get beautiful.

➣ Go to lunch and practice flirt techniques.

➣ Go shopping. Flirt.

➣ Change into flirty evening attire.

➣ Bar hop. Flirt.

➣ Have dinner at a great restaurant. Flirt.

➣ Get home safely.

Great Man

Girl time is so important. I want all of you to bond over great food and to talk incessantly about men. It's fun and good for the spirit. Now it's time to pass out blank "Great Man" profiles to your friends. Encourage everyone to share their answers with the group. "Hello, my name is Sally and I'm looking for a great man who . . ." Laugh and drink a bit more champagne.

Wing Woman

Now that everyone knows what they're looking for in a man, work together to devise a plan of action. These are now your wing women and you are theirs. Make a pact to help each other meet men, to never fight over a man, and to always be there for each other. If Susie wants to go out Friday night but doesn't have anyone to go out with, get off the sofa, make yourself beautiful and be her wing woman. Who knows, you just might get lucky that night as well.

Gym

Now head for the gym—all of you. If your friends don't belong to your gym, go online and download free passes for them. Most gyms offer at least a day or two for free. If yours doesn't, see if they can buy one-day passes.

You can all stick together or split up and flirt. If you go it alone, scan the room until you see a man working out alone. That's your opportunity to get close to him. Get on the equipment next to him and fiddle with it for a minute, then ask him how to use it. He'll happily show you what to do and if he's interested, he'll strike up a conversation. Score!

If you stick together (chickens!), do 30 minutes of cardio on the treadmill, a stationary bike, or on an elliptical trainer, followed by 30 minutes of weight training. Help each other with new moves. Incorporate lunges and crunches. The hour will go by faster than you can imagine. Stay longer, if you like.

The most-effective encouragement comes from working out with a personal trainer. Knowing you're paying for the session will definitely force you to work harder so you can get your money's worth. Trainers are expensive, especially if you use one the recommended three times a week, which is why I want to help you build a support team for you to work out with.

When the hour is over and everyone is feeling invigorated, invite your friends to become your work-out buddies. Devise a schedule that is realistic and keep each other motivated to stay on target. The more women in your group, the better. This way, when someone bails—and they will—you will still have someone to work out with.

Shower

I hope you remembered to bring your gym bag and a change of clothes. It's easier for everyone to shower and get ready at the gym than it is at your house. Do your hair and makeup with the awareness that you may run into a hot guy. Remember, you always want to look your best—no pony tails today. Dab on a hint of perfume, swipe on a bit more lip gloss and head out. You look marvelous!

NOON
Ladies Who Lunch

Pick a happening place—somewhere where businessmen go for power lunches. Then order wine or bottled water and healthy meals for you and your friends. You don't want to undo your hard work at the gym by indulging in pasta and bread. I want you light on your feet for the remainder of the day and into the night.

Have fun, gossip, and most of all, flirt. Pull out your book and teach your friends your new flirt techniques. Let go of your inhibitions and show them how it's done. Become the teacher and watch your confidence grow.

Encourage each one of your friends to take a stab at flirting with a handsome stranger. But don't be too obvious about it. If there's just two or three of you, go to the ladies room, leaving one to flirt. Watch her in action and watch his reaction, but only if you can do so without being discovered. If there's a huge group of you, two or three of you should go to the restroom and the rest engage in a conversation that doesn't include the lady on deck. Let her work her magic, then turn your attention back to her.

All of you are practicing for tonight so don't worry about actually connecting with a man right now. If the opportunity presents itself, go for it, but don't focus on it. Right now you're building confidence. Enjoy.

Retail Therapy

Take an hour or so just to shop, shop, shop, and shop some more. You don't have to buy anything, just play. Try on clothes and shoes, jewelry and purses, just for fun. This is your down time, so relax and indulge. Flirt with the cute shoe salesman. Let him pamper you and make you feel like a princess. Shopping is therapeutic for women, whether you make a purchase or simply pretend that you can. This is also a good exercise in dream building. Coveting things out of your reach will motivate you to work harder to get what you want.

NIGHT

Out On The Town

Go home and relax for a while. After you change into your stunning outfits, freshen up, and get out there. Feel free to bar hop before you go to dinner. Practice flirting everywhere you go and when you've flirted with everyone worth flirting with, go somewhere else.

Choose an upscale restaurant for dinner. It's always a good idea to surround yourself with successful people, and high-end establishments are usually full of them. Go all out. Order wine, appetizers, salads, entrées, and dessert—and tip very well. All too often, women are seen skimping on meals or trying to ride other people's tabs. Don't be one of those women. I understand not everyone can afford such an extravagance, but do it anyway. Just don't do it often. Taste the good life so you become hungry for it.

People will notice your table: women gathered together enjoying a fine dinner and each other's company. That's intriguing. A strong, confident man will send a bottle of wine your way. Accept it and savor every drop. Don't worry about trying to figure out who he has his eye on. It will become obvious—it's whomever the waiter speaks to about the wine. If that lucky lady is you, kindly locks eyes with the generous man, give him a smile, mouth thank you, and leave it at that—for now. When your meal is finished and it's time to go, separate from the pack and go over to personally thank him for his generosity. Your friends should give you a few minutes alone and if all is going well, they can join you. Hopefully, he has friends for them to talk to.

It's perfectly acceptable to go to the bar for a cocktail after dinner. If you've exhausted all the male options at this location, go to a ritzy hotel bar. There's almost always available men to talk to. Just be cautious, as a lot of them will be married men on business trips. Stay clear and focus on single men who could lead to potential dates. I hope you had fun. Be careful getting home and if anyone has had too much to drink, hire a cab. Good night!

Finished

Well, you made it. You survived five challenging days of Flirt Boot Camp. You trained yourself to eat better, to exercise more often, and to broaden your horizons by reading the newspaper. You learned new flirting techniques and put them into practice. You learned how to approach men and how to draw them to you. You bonded with friends. And best of all, you had fun.

If you have followed this course 100 percent, you will have met a man and arranged to go out on a date. Even if you followed just some of the techniques, you may have landed a date. It's all within your power. You control your dating destiny.

Chapter Quiz

Have You Mastered the Art of Flirting or Do You Need to Go Back to Flirt Boot Camp?

1. When you see a hot guy you:
   A. Walk right up to him, tell him he's hot, and ask him out.
   B. Make eye contact, smile and look away—knowing he'll be by your side in a matter of minutes.
   C. Avoid him. You're too shy to talk to someone so good looking.

2. Your best flirting technique is:
   A. To maintain an open stance even in a crowded room. You're approachable.
   B. Grabbing a man's butt.
   C. Stating the obvious—I want you to ask me out.

3. A skilled flirt knows:
   A. How to be seductive not slutty, available not desperate and poised not stiff.
   B. How to get any man away from any woman.
   C. That overt sexuality is the key to attracting a man.

4. A woman should send a man a drink when:
   A. Hell freezes over.
   B. He's ignored her other advances and gestures—if at first you don't succeed, try, try again.
   C. The rare opportunity presents itself and it just feels like the right thing to do.

5. Playing with your hair, crossing and uncrossing your legs, and batting your eyelashes are all:
    A. Annoying things that girls do to attract men.
    B. Not part of your repertoire.
    C. Signs of flirting.

6. You ask a man for the time because:
    A. You want to know what time it is.
    B. You're attracted to him and want to meet him.
    C. You want to steal his watch.

7. To be a good flirt you:
    A. Read books with flirting techniques, practice at home and test your skills in public—on handsome men.
    B. Come on to your best friend's boyfriend to prove how talented you are.
    C. Get a job as an exotic dancer to learn from the pros.

8. Flirting with another man in front of your date:
    A. Will make him jealous and like you all the more.
    B. Creates just the right amount of drama to make your night more interesting.
    C. Is disrespectful and not something you do.

9. When your date flirts with another woman you:
    A. Throw a fit and storm out crying.
    B. Don't say a word. You finish the evening and don't grant him another date.
    C. Try to one up him by flirting with the waiter, the bartender, and any other man who crosses your path—even the guy at the table next to yours despite his wife sitting beside him.

10. Flirting is:

   A. Not something you're very good at so you don't do it.

   B. The backbone of your existence. You flirt with just about anyone to make yourself feel attractive even if that means you have to step on other women's toes now and again—all is fair in love and flirting.

   C. Something you do to make other people feel good about themselves, which makes you feel good too. Plus, it's a lot of fun!

Your Results

You may consider yourself an expert flirt if you chose the following answers

1. **B.** Sending signals lets a man know you're interested and invites him to talk to you. You will meet a lot of men this way.

2. **A.** Your ability to stand out in a crowd will improve your chances of meeting new suitors.

3. **A.** Your outward appearance will determine the type of men you attract—and yours speaks to quality men exclusively.

4. **C.** This is not a tactic you use often, but one which yields great results when handled properly.

5. **C.** Being coy and utterly feminine is a fun way to let a man know you're interested in him.

6. **B.** Not one to be too forward, you use non-threatening questions to break the ice and put the ball back in his court.

7. **A.** You are an ambitious woman who strives to be the best at whatever she does—at work, at home and most definitely, at play.

8. **C.** You are confident and secure and don't feel the need to use childish tactics to get a man's attention. He will be so relieved.

9. **B.** You don't see the need to stoop to his level. He'll learn soon enough when he realizes his actions cost him you.

10. **C.** Your dance card is full because you aren't afraid to flirt, flirt, and flirt some more.

   Congratulations! You have mastered the art of flirting.
   What are you waiting for? Go flirt.

Chapter 6

Sex and the Single Girl

Secret #6: Be Upfront About Where You Stand Sexually

*The human race has been set up. Someone, somewhere, is playing
a practical joke on us. Apparently, women need to
feel loved to have sex. Men need to have sex
to feel loved. How do we ever get started?*
—Billy Connolly

Sex is a taboo subject for some and on the tip of the tongue
for so many others. How do we know what's right and what's
wrong when it comes to sex—morally, personally, and even
socially? This is a challenging question and one which deserves some time and thought. Let's not rush through this.

First of all, I'd like to say that there really is no right or wrong; there's only a right for you, or a wrong for you. I don't believe religion or society should make that choice for you. These should merely be used as guides to help you make an informed decision. A consenting adult should be able to make whatever decision makes sense for her, without religious or social ramifications. However, that's not the world we live in, now is it?

With that in mind, let's explore our options. A single woman can choose to remain abstinent until marriage—a practice that is commendable in theory but not very realistic or attainable. She can refrain from sex until she's in a committed relationship, a practice that is not only commendable but attainable. Or she can throw caution (and her panties) to the wind and do as she damn well pleases, a practice that is frowned upon by religion and society and mom and dad.

DOING WITHOUT

If abstinence is your chosen practice, you should revel in it and make the most of it. We all know men want what they can't have, so drive him nuts. He'll put you on a pedestal and pursue you with undying conviction (though he might sleep with your roommate in the mean time). Never compromise your principals. No ring, no nookie, no exception.

MONOGAMOUS SEX

Monogamous sex is a happy medium when you and your man are serious about one another. Your church may not give you its blessings, but society will certainly nod with approval. Embracing this practice will keep the men interested in you for many reasons: He will want what he can't have (not yet, anyway). He will respect you for being selective. He will appreciate the fact that you haven't slept with every Tom, Dick, and Harry in town. Most of all, he will respect you for standing by your principles—even as he's begging you to give in.

TIMING IS EVERYTHING

Now it's time to focus on more practical things, like when to sleep with him, how to bring up the topic of condoms and STDs, and all the other not-so-lovely issues associated with non-marital sex. Notice how I didn't say, "pre-marital." Who's to say you will ever want to get married?

Men want to sleep with you on the first date. That's no secret, we all know this. What a lot of women *don't* know is that even though men are just itching to get in your pants on the first date, they will become more intrigued with you if you don't.

A one-night stand got its name for a reason—it's a single night of sex and nothing more. If you sleep with a man on the first date, you can believe me when I tell you that there won't be a second. If you have no interest in seeing this man again, then by all means, go right ahead and do him. But if you do want a second, or even a third and fourth date, it's best to wait. No matter how cute he is, no matter how horny you are.

THE OLD DRY RUB

Date your new guy for at least a few weeks before you get naked with him. It's time to revert back to those high school days of heavy petting and kissing. Let me paint a picture for

TOP 10 MALE EROGENOUS ZONES

1. Scalp	6. Inner Thighs
2. Ears	7. Glans (Head of penis)
3. Lips	8. Perineum
4. Neck	9. Scrotum
5. Chest	10. Buttocks

you: Wrap your legs around Mr. Wonderful and gently kiss his neck. Work your way up to his earlobes and finally, explore his lips ever so lightly. Kiss him softly, sweetly, and as your passion for one another grows, part his lips and teach him the fine art of French kissing.

Allow him to lie on top of you on the sofa and let him explore your body while you remain dressed. No matter how hot and bothered you become, you must not give in to temptation. As a courtesy (yes, you're *always* gracious), warn him that there will be no skin-on-skin contact just yet. Let him know that you want to get comfortable with his body and his touch, first. He won't mind. In fact, he'll love it. It will give him something to look forward to. Now that you're comfortable with each other and you're confident he's not just after one thing, you can take it to the next level. His hand on your bare skin will feel like heaven to both of you, even more so now than if you had rushed into it. Always remember, we value most what is hardest to get. So don't just play hard to get; *be* hard to get.

HAPPY ENDING

Your clothes are strewn around the house, you're enjoying being naked with your guy, but you're just not ready to have sex. That's perfectly okay. There are a lot of other pleasurable things you can do without penetration.

For example, you can engage in mutual masturbation. If he's shy (fat chance!) you can lead the way by touching yourself first and letting him watch you pleasure yourself. Then take his hand and place it between your thighs. If he knows what he's doing, this can be as climatic as full-blown sex. If he's not as skilled as you'd like him to be, teach him. Show him what you like and then return the favor.

ALL THE WAY

Once you're ready to go all the way with a man, let go of your inhibitions and just enjoy. Sex is a wonderful thing—it's meant to bond men and women, and to bring tremendous pleasure. Granted, first-time sex isn't always the most pleasurable sex and it doesn't always bring two people together, but in time, and with a lot of practice, it can. So practice until you get it right, and then try something new, and practice *that* until you get it right. Continue to try new and exciting things until arthritis sets in and you can no longer wrap both legs behind your head. You get the picture.

PANDORA'S BOX

It's time to address that monthly challenge we all face—a visit from Aunt Flow. She means well, but damn it, sex just isn't the same with her in the room. What's a horny girl to do? Do what you're most comfortable with. Whether you refrain or engage is up to the both of you. Is your man the squeamish type? He may want to sit this one out. Or is he a naughty boy who gets turned on by it? He should be made aware so he can enjoy the moment even more. Don't keep your period a secret. Any man who has ever had a girlfriend knows what a tampon is and what it's used for. Embrace your femininity. Slide a towel between you and the sheets, and do what nature intended.

TECHNIQUE

A man's ego is directly linked to two main things—his job per-formance and his sexual performance. Make a man feel like a great lover and he will feel like the king of the world—and fall head over heels for you.

TOP 10 FEMALE EROGENOUS ZONES	
1. Breasts	6. Back
2. Clitoris	7. Legs
3. Ears	8. Buttocks
4. Lips	9. Feet
5. Neck	10. Hands & Arms

Being good in bed isn't so much about swinging from the chandelier as it is about making your partner feel satisfied. Find out what he likes and pleasure him that way. Don't worry so much about trying *Cosmopolitan*'s latest trick. Save that for the day when the initial attraction has worn off and you need a little pick-me-up.

Speaking of tricks, guys are often intimidated by girls with goody drawers full of Jack Rabbits and whips, so keep your drawer closed and the whips where they belong—out of site. Pull out your prettiest lingerie and scented candles, instead. This is what will set him on fire (and I don't mean literally). In the beginning, show him your sweet, feminine side and give him a chance to spoil you. That's what he really wants to do any-how, to please you.

I'm not saying you need to be a little Miss Innocent, just keep the S&M to a minimum. You can be a good lover—no, scratch that, a *great* lover—just by being attentive. Spend time running your hands all over his body. Massage his back and work your way around to his front, kissing him from head to toe. He's probably not used to getting so much attention and will enjoy every second of it. Make love to him whether you're in love or not; this will leave a lasting impression and have him aching for more.

WEARING A RAINCOAT

A lot of men hate wearing a condom; they say it takes away from their pleasure or that they can't "finish," if they're wearing one. Oh well, that's not exactly your problem, now is it? There's no easy way to tell them, so just say it directly: I never have sex without a condom." This is a mood-killing subject so address it before the main event. You could argue that if you're using birth control pills, have both been tested for sexually-transmitted diseases and are in a committed, monogamous relationship, there's no need for a condom. But you're still at risk! I believe you should still use a condom.

Now that we agree that a condom is always necessary, we must address technique. Who's going to put it on him? This is totally up to you, but I think it is kind of sexy to put it on for him because it helps keep him in the mood. If you're nervous or don't know how, ask him to teach you. He won't say no, and you'll have fun learning.

Just be sure to replace the condom periodically. If he's into marathon sex (lucky you!), he's going to need a fresh condom from time to time. Take this opportunity to

PHONE SEX

Dear Jula,
I travel a lot for work and as a result, my sex life has suffered. I found a perfect solution, though—phone sex. I love passing the time in a lonely hotel room by burning up the phone lines with dirty talk. It's almost as good as the real thing. I just started dating someone new and haven't mentioned my penchant for phone sex. How can I bring it up without him thinking I'm kinky or strange?

Delores

Dear Delores,
Phone sex is perfectly healthy and nothing to be ashamed of. I'm sure this new guy will be thrilled to join in on the fun. The next time you're out of town and the urge strikes, call him up and gradually start a sensual conversation. "I wish you were laying here next to me," or "What are you wearing?" These lines will let him know what's on your mind without you coming right out and saying, "Let's have phone sex."

Jula Jane

let some of your other skills shine through. Give him a few kisses below the belt and then wrap him back up like a present. Merry Christmas to you!

A word of caution: some men will agree to wear a condom in the beginning and later try to convince you that it's not necessary. In the heat of the moment you will want to give in, but don't. If he presses, kiss him on the forehead and say, "That's okay, baby, we can always do something else. I think *Beaches* is on TBS." He'll have that condom on so fast and he won't ever suggest that he not use a condom—at least not tonight.

HAVE VIRUS, WILL TRAVEL

Even though it makes me cringe just to type the words—sexually transmitted disease—I'm going to talk about it. It has to be addressed. After all, this is a book about dating and with dating comes sex, and with sex comes the risk of STDs.

I'm not a doctor so I'm not going to take a clinical approach here; I'm merely going to touch on the social aspect of it. When you have sex you run the risk of contracting a sexually-transmitted disease, or STD. Like it or not, protected or not, tested or not, it's possible.

And it's even possible to contract diseases when you don't have intercourse. Without getting too graphic or too clinical, let me give you an example: Your one-night stand, or your boyfriend of three months, or your husband of 16 years, has a cold sore on his lip. Being the giver that he is, he delights you with 25 minutes of oral pleasure. Well, Happy Birthday, you just got more than you bargained for—a "cold sore" down under. Does that make you a bad person? No. Does that make him a bad person? No. But it does place you both in the same boat, without a paddle or a cure.

The point is, even the most innocent connection can result in unwanted consequences. How, then, do we date and have sex when the risk is so high? Carefully and intelligently, that's how. Choose your hook-ups wisely. One-night stands may not be a moral issue for you, but what about the horror of contracting a disease from a man you're never going to see again? Hey, thanks for the Chlamydia. Have a nice life. Think about the consequences of your actions before it's too late because frankly, some STDs last a lifetime—or end your life.

Spending time getting to know someone before you become intimate with them could save you from a lifetime of open sores. Then again, it could not. Many people do not know they have a STD, and others know, but won't tell you. You could be together five years and never know, or for five passionate minutes and know right away. Sex is a gamble. Period.

If you do become an STD statistic, don't beat yourself up. You're not alone. STDs affect 55 million Amerians—1 in 4—and each year, 12 million new cases are diagnosed. But you will have to decide whether or not to share the news with future partners. Obviously, the right thing to do is to tell someone if you currently have a contagious disease. If it's a thing of the past that won't affect him, keep it to yourself, if you wish.

Whatever you do, don't bring it up on your first date. You may decide you don't want to see him again, so why reveal such an intimate fact about yourself for no reason? When you're ready to sleep with someone, bring it up a few days before. I can't think of a bigger turn-off during sex than the sudden revelation, "Oh, by the way, my gonorrhea finally cleared up but my warts are back."

BASHFUL

Dear Jula,
I hate undressing in front of a guy. In fact, I hate being naked in front of a guy with the lights on, ever. I'm just not comfortable with my body. I worry about him thinking I'm too fat and that my thighs are too big and my breasts, too small. I want to loosen up but I don't know how. Any advice for a bashful girl?
Cassandra

Dear Cassandra,
Perfect bodies are out, sexy swaggers are in. A recent study shows that men are more likely to be drawn to women who have a sexy swagger? This means you must work more on your confidence and less on your abs. Strut your stuff and drive him wild.
Jula Jane

WHAM, BAM ... YOU KNOW THE REST

"What does it mean when a guy sleeps with you and never calls you again?" It means he suckered you into sleeping with him.

Men don't associate sex with emotion, at least not nearly as much as women do. A guy can sleep with a woman and never give her another thought. Keep that in mind when you're about to hook up with someone. This may be the last time you see him.

Here's the traditional dance: You meet a guy and he comes on strong. He takes you out to dinner, goes out of his way to see you and calls and texts you all the time. On the fifth date, you sleep with him. He calls the next day but doesn't make another date until the weekend. This time, you don't go to dinner—it's straight to his place. You sleep together several times that night and again in the morning. He kisses you and sends you on your way.

A whole day passes and there's no word from your new lover, so you text and you call. No response. Another 24 hours pass and still no word, so you text and you text. Finally, he responds. He's nonchalant and noncommittal. "I've been swamped at work. Let's get together soon," he tells you.

"Soon" turns into three weeks. You're hurt and angry and yet you go running to him when he says, "Come over." You pack your bag (in case he lets you spend the night) and race over to his house. You ring the bell, but he's not there, so you wait in your car. Before you know it, 45 minutes have passed. Suddenly you see him coming towards you. "Sorry babe, I grabbed a drink with the guys and lost track of time." He smiles and all is forgiven.

This scenario is typical with men who practice casual sex. He pursues you in the beginning to see if he can get you in bed, and once he does, he quickly loses interest. And yet he keeps you hanging on by sending an occasional text and by hooking up with you now and again. This way, he knows he can have a booty call whenever he wants it. The fact of the matter is his prime focus has shifted away from you and onto his next conquest.

Don't hate him for this behavior. He knows that if he spends too much time with you, you will start to believe you're his girl-friend, which you're not. Women tend to assume commitment when they sleep with a man, or spend more than two days a week with him. In the above scenario, his actions are speaking loud and clear: if it's commitment you want, it's a different guy you need.

Sex without love is merely exercise.
—Robert A. Heinlein

MULTIPLE PARTNERS

Just as a single man has the right to date several women, a single woman has the right to date several men; after all, she's single. This also means she has the right to sleep with as many men as she likes, without any commitments. What she doesn't have the right to do is to lie and endanger her partners. If you're sleeping with more than one guy, don't tell him he's the only one, especially if you're having unprotected sex. It's important that as women, we are upfront about our choices so our partners can make informed decisions. In other words, if John knew you had just crawled out of Mike's bed and into his, he may choose to pass on the oral feast he had planned for you. Then again, he may not. Give him the choice; you'd want the same courtesy.

Since we're talking about multiple partners, I find it appropri-ate to address threesomes. This can be two men and one woman, or more commonly, two women and one man. As I always say, "To each their own." If you and your guy want to experiment by bringing a third person into your bed, then go for it. Just be careful. This sort of thing can go south very quickly and before you know it, someone's jealous. It may be

you who is jealous of your man with another woman, or your man might become
jealous of you with another man—or
another woman.

Another side effect of the threesome is
that his opinion of you will probably
change. He might be as involved in the
act as you are, but that doesn't mean he
won't condemn *you* for it. Regardless, you
risk ruining a good thing for one night of
erotic exploration. Give it careful consideration before you go down this road.

WHAT'S GOOD FOR THE GOOSE

I know what you're thinking: men do it all
the time. They date and sleep with multiple partners, they keep silent about their
diseases, and they lie to get you in bed.
You're right. That doesn't make it right
and that doesn't mean you should do it,
too. Treat men how you yourself want to
be treated, and in the long run you'll
come out on top (pun intended).

A single woman can enjoy a happy,
healthy, adventurous sex life if she's honest with herself and her partners—and re-
spects herself and her partners. You don't
have to follow anyone else's rules. Just do
what's right for you.

Chapter Quiz

Are You the Master of Your Sexuality?

1. When it comes to sex you:
   A. Are responsible, adventurous and considerate.
   B. Can't get enough of it. You're up for anything that brings you pleasure.
   C. Are intimidated, inhibited and utterly petrified.

2. The thing you fear the most about sex is:
   A. Forgetting how to use all the toys you bought.
   B. Contracting a disease.
   C. A man thinking you're not good in bed.

3. When a man asks you to sleep with him for the first time you:
   A. Do as he asks, whether you're ready or not—you don't want to offend him.
   B. Go for it—if you like him, have had the sex baggage talk, and have a condom.
   C. Turn him down flat. You're not that easy.

4. You hate dealing with the condom issue so you:
   A. Don't. You have sex sans condom and hope for the best.
   B. Avoid sex. You kiss and pet and break up with him when it's time to go all the way.
   C. Give yourself a pep talk before uttering those five incredibly important words—do you have a condom?

5. If a man has the guts to tell you about a looming STD you:
   A. Thank him for his honesty and stand by your man—warts and all.
   B. Freak out and never speak to him again.
   C. Pretend that it doesn't bother you and slowly phase him out of your life.

6. Safe sex is:
   A. An oxymoron. There's no such thing as safe sex.
   B. Attainable if you always use a condom, get tested regularly and maintain an open line of communication with your partner.
   C. A nuisance that gets in the way of free love.

7. The morning after a one-night stand you:
   A. Get dressed, do the dreaded walk of shame, and vow never to do it again.
   B. Tell him that you don't normally do this and ask him to call you sometime, which you both know he'll never do.
   C. Take a hot shower, grab a cup of coffee and start your day. You don't expect him to call so you don't dwell on it. And besides, you have more important things to do—like shop for a fabulous new pair of shoes.

8. When a man is having performance issues between the sheets you:
   A. Make fun of him, get dressed and leave.
   B. Take the focus off of him by putting it on to you. You encourage him to pleasure you orally, which drives him wild and inevitably solves his problem.
   C. Take it personally and pout until he finally rises to the occasion.

9. If you're not in a monogamous relationship and are sexually active you:
   A. Let your partners know that you are sleeping with other men and that you practice safe sex.
   B. Do as you please and keep the details to yourself—it's none of their business.
   C. Tell each man that you sleep with that he's the only one so he won't think you're promiscuous.

10. A man invites you on a long romantic weekend the very same weekend you're supposed to start your period. You:

A. Go anyway and let the tampons fall where they may.

B. Cancel because the thought of him finding out that you have your period is too embarrassing.

C. Let him know how much you're looking forward to this trip, then explain that the timing isn't as in sync with your body as it is with your mind.

Your Results

You can consider yourself sexually knowledgeable and sexually responsible if you chose these answers:

1. **A.** You embrace your sexuality with zest and caution. Bravo!

2. **B.** You're a well-informed woman who knows how to avoid an unwanted pregnancy—with birth control pills and condoms—and you're smart enough to realize that no matter how careful you are, you're always at risk for contracting an unwanted disease.

3. **B.** As a confident woman, you follow your libido as you see fit. You don't have time for silly games, and you never allow yourself to be persuaded into something you're not ready for.

4. **C.** You realize that you won't die from embarrassment if you ask a man to wear a condom—but you could die, in fact, if you don't use one.

5. **A.** You don't run from adversity—you face it head on because you know that one day you, too, could be faced with such a challenge.

6. **B.** Practicing safe sex is something you do to protect yourself and your partners because the alternative is too daunting—and frankly, it's not something you're willing to subject yourself to.

7. **C.** You take a one-night stand for what it is—one night of sex. You don't have unrealistic expectations and therefore, you don't feel let down when he doesn't call.

8. **B.** A smart woman knows not to stomp on a man's sexual ego and you are definitely a smart woman. Helping him get over his problem without talking about it endears him to you.

9. **A.** Sex is not something you lie about—it's too dangerous and it's not a game you're willing to play. After all, you wouldn't want someone to play that game with you.

10. **C.** You aren't ashamed of your period, but you do feel it's important to be upfront about it, just in case it puts a damper on what would otherwise be a wonderful weekend.

Chapter 7

Check Out His Package

Secret #7: Do a Little Digging to Get Some Real Lovin'

*Truth is like the sun. You can shut it out
for a time, but it ain't goin' away.*
—Elvis Presley

A girl has a right to know what she's getting herself into, so I say look long and look hard at a man's package before you invest too much time in him. Who wants to devote six weeks to stroking an ego and laughing at silly jokes, only to learn the package is, well, let's just say it doesn't quite measure up.

Life is short and should be lived to the absolute fullest. Don't waste precious time on small packages when a *big* package is staring you in the face. Grab it and enjoy the ride—you deserve it.

WHAT'S IN HIS PACKAGE?

A man's package is made up of many things: genes, personality, education, career, finances, hobbies, family, friends, and plans for the future. You must dissect these and figure out what he's made of without him knowing what you're up to.

Your title: Special Agent Bond, Jane Bond

Your assignment: To get the mark to talk without getting caught.

GENES

You need to find out if your Great Man has good genes. Why? Because you want to know how long "until death do us part" really is. Are we talking 20 great years or 50? If his great-great-grandfather lived to be 95 and his great-grandfather lived to be 102 and his father is 83 and still lifting weights, you're probably looking at doing a lot of time with this man. That's great news if you love him and never fall out of love with him, but it's not such great news if you're after his fortune.

All kidding aside, it's not a bad idea to know his family medical history for many reasons: One, if cancer runs in his family, he has a higher probability of being diagnosed with it, and you will have to take care of him one day, Two, if he's schizophrenic and Dr. Jekyll neglected to introduce you to Mr. Hyde, it'll show up in a medical analysis, and three, if you plan to have children and he's a potential sperm donor, you'll want to know what's in your baby's gene pool.

Begin your research by asking him leading questions like, "Does your dog talk to you?" If he says yes, you know he's got a bit of mental history in his otherwise sexy jeans, I mean *genes.* Then take him on a trip down memory lane; he's bound to reveal bits of information that will help determine your future. Continue down this path until you're fully informed and ready to make a decision—to stay or not to stay.

PERSONALITY

A man doesn't always let his true personality shine through at first. Frequently, in the beginning stages of dating, he'll show you a side to him that isn't really him. It's his alter ego, Johnny Good Guy. Johnny Good Guy likes to take walks in the park and listen to classical music. He's kind and sincere, he's patient and attentive, and he loves children.

Ninety days into your coupling, Johnny Good Guy disappears and Johnny Come Lately steps in. Johnny Come Lately likes to take walks in the park—with your sister—and he likes to listen to metal bands and play air guitar. Sexy! His idea of "sincere" is not letting the door hit you where the good Lord split you. He is patient—patient while you cook his dinner. And he's attentive. Well, I guess copping a feel can be considered attentive. Oh, and his views on children? It's barefoot and pregnant for you; hanging out and drinking beer for him.

The point is, don't fall for a guy until you really get to know him. The first 90 days are basically fake; he's smitten, you're smitten, and neither one of you is real. Let those 90 days go by then evaluate his true personality as it starts to emerge.

IVY LEAGUE
LOSER

Dear Jula,
I've been dating a guy who can't tell the truth. He lies about everything: where he's from, where he went to school, what he does for a living, and so on and so on. We haven't been together very long, just six months, but it's been long enough for me to fall in love with him. I don't know what to do. I love him, but who exactly is it that I love—the real him or the man he led me to believe he is?
Julie

Dear Julie,
You're in love with a fictitious man. The real question is should you stay or should you go. Give him another chance, this time with your eyes open. Try to see the real man behind the lies and then decide if you still love him. If you do, forgive his bull and put it behind you. But don't ever forget his lying ways. If he lied about who he is, he'll lie about other things too. Can you spend a lifetime with that?
Jula Jane

EDUCATION

"I graduated from Harvard and went on to study at Stanford." This may sound like music to your ears as it rolls off his blue-blooded tongue, but it just might not be true.

What, a man lie? Do your homework. If he said he went to Yale, get on the phone with Yale and find out. If he said he went to the state university, drive down there and dig through their records.

Men like to beat their chests and pump up their egos by telling tall tales about who they are and where they come from. Their education is no exception. He'll tell you he has a Ph.D. when all he really has is a certificate from a vocational school. He thinks you won't make him prove it; prove him wrong. "A Ph.D., that's quite impressive. I'd love to see your diploma sometime. I bet it's hanging proudly on your wall." Now he has to put up or shut up, or make a lame excuse, which you won't buy. "I'd love to show it to you but I gave it to my mother as a gift and she lives in Timbuktu," might be his reply. But you know what's going on. Liar!

Love is an irresistible desire
to be irresistibly desired.
—Robert Frost

You may not think his education matters at this stage in the game, but it does. If he leads you to believe he's highly educated, you'll think he's capable of earning a lofty income. How are you going to feel 12 months later when you're in love with him and discover he only has a GED?

I'm not suggesting a man without an education isn't worth dating. I'm just saying that he needs to be upfront in the beginning so you can have a realistic expectation of what life with him will be like. Then you can make a decision about whether or not to date him. Take everything he says with a grain of salt and know that he added just a bit of pepper for taste.

CAREER

"I'm dating a doctor." "He's a lawyer." "John's an investment banker." Mom and dad will be so proud and all your friends will turn green with envy. Why? Because your man is successful, that's why. And a woman who nabs a successful man is considered well, successful.

Does this all really matter? Isn't love more important than anything else? Yes and no. Yes, this all really matters and no, love isn't more important than anything else, at least not in the real world. And sister, like it or not, you're living in the real world.

The idealist in you: the person who falls in love with a boy of 38, who still lives with his mommy, wants to believe he'll grow up and make something of himself—if not for him, for you. I hate to be the bearer of bad news, but Peter Pan will never grow up. He may get pushed out of the nest one day but he'll fall into another cushy den—yours. Your little darling will allow you to mother him, to pay the bills, put a roof over his head, support his habits (comic books and video games) and wash his Spiderman undies. Isn't he cute? No!

Sexist or not, I'm going to say it. A woman should not support a man. There I said it; let the e-mails begin. A man needs to stand on his own two feet, get a job, and work hard at building a life and a future for himself and his future family. There's no excuse for a lazy man and there's even less of an excuse for a woman who supports a lazy man.

A man's self-esteem is directly connected to his career and his ability to make money. He feels pride when he gets a check and is able to take care of the ones he loves. Don't take that away from him. Don't be his crutch, be his partner. Give him support through encouragement, not by handing him an allowance.

Some men are sneaky. Your new guy may tell you he works in a big-time law firm and is slated to become partner in the next two years, when the truth is he's in research at the aforementioned big-time law firm and can't seem to pass the bar. No, not the bar exam, the bar—the old-school tavern located just around the corner from his apartment. The very same tavern where he's known as the beer-meister, Joe Cool, Mr. Dart Man, and his favorite, Flame Thrower. I'd rather not explain how he got that nickname. I will say it has something to do with flatulence and a lighter. You figure it out.

Jane Bond's no fool. She'll smile sweetly and feign an, oh-so-impressed look on her face when the new guy brags about what he does. Then she'll check out his story. I've been forced to become Jane Bond before. Once I met a man in Las Vegas who told me he created True Religion Jeans and was the acting CEO. He spent a lot of money that night on champagne (Veuve Clicquot) and limos (from Caesar's to the Wynn). He even gave my girlfriends money when they lost at the blackjack table. He talked a good talk and seemed to walk the walk, but I didn't buy it, not 100 percent, anyhow.

We exchanged contact information and called it a night. (I'm a good girl). The next day after I flew home, I checked out my new man. It was really quite simple. I Googled "True Religion Brand Jeans," pulled up their website, clicked on investor relations and searched for his name. "Hmm, that's odd," I thought to myself. "Someone else's name is posted next to the title CEO." So I looked further down the list. Perhaps he's the CFO. Nope. COO? Nope. President? Nope. Who is he then? Further investigation (a phone call to the company) revealed that on that fun-filled night in Vegas, I had met—brace yourself—a *sales rep!* I can see how he mistook his position for founder and CEO, can't you? *Not!* Oh well, I had a fun night and I got two cool pairs of jeans out of the deal since he did follow up on his promise to send the latest designs to me.

This could've gone bad, though. Had I not checked out his story and discovered he was a fraud, I would've flown back to Las Vegas to meet him for the heavy weight fight, as we planned, and I may have let things go a bit further this time. I *decided* I wasn't up for a long-distance affair with a poser. The bottom line? When it comes to a man's career, make sure he has one, and make sure he has the one he says he has.

FINANCES

Every man you meet is going to fudge a little about how much cash he has in the bank. You may not ask, but he's going to tell. This is his way of impressing you. He's not thinking about the consequences. He's thinking about getting in your pants.

"Yeah, I just wired a hundred grand to my broker today. He got a lead on something big and since I'm his best client, he let me in on it first." Are you impressed? You may not mean to be, but you probably are. You're thinking, "If he's able to wire a hundred grand for an investment, he must have a lot more where that came from." Think again.

I wish I could say men with money don't flaunt it, but that's no longer true. All men flaunt money, whether they have it or not, simply for the fact that it gets them laid. Listen with both ears when he spells out just how rich he is, and then call him on it when he least expects it. Don't get in his face and demand to know the truth. He'll never rat himself out. Instead, be cunning: "Have you had much luck with the TRLG stock?"

FACT CHECKER

Dear Jula,
I just met a man who seems too good to be true. How can I find out if he really is who he says he is?
Elisa

Dear Elisa,
Background check. That's right, run a background check on him. Look into his past, his present, and his future. Does he have a criminal record? You can check. Does he have a wife? You can find out. Did he really play pro ball in college? I don't know, but his transcripts sure do. The information you want is out there. You just have to go get it.
Jula Jane

When he looks at you like you're crazy, you'll know he was full of it and he doesn't remember his own lie.

The best way to distinguish fact from fiction is to look for discrepancies. It's hard to keep up with so many lies; he will slip up now and again and when he does, make a mental note of it. This isn't about being sneaky or tricking men; it's about getting to the truth. Once you have the truth, the whole truth, and nothing but the truth, you'll be able to make a sound decision as to whether or not this man is a good match for you.

HOBBIES

It's good to learn about a man's hobbies, so you can see if you will fit into his life. An avid golfer may want you by his side from tee to tee. Then again, he may not. You need to know which way he swings so you'll know if you need to take up golfing, or take up with a boy toy. After all, a girl has needs. A work-out junkie spends his early mornings and late evenings in the gym. Are you up for getting sweaty? Are you ready to be a health nut, eat right and wear muscle-flaunting clothes? If not, you may need to find a different guy.

The hobbies and interests of the guy you're dating will impact your life, be it time spent together or apart. Find out what he likes to do and decide if it's something you're willing to do with him, willing to let him do without you, or unwilling to deal with at all. You already play second fiddle to his work. Are you willing to play third string to his hobby?

FAMILY

When you date a man you aren't necessarily in a relationship with his family, as is the case when you're married. But you are linked. He may want you to meet his folks one day, when things are getting serious between you. Then again, he may not and won't that piss you off? Women tend to judge their relationships on a multitude of factors, and meeting his family is a big one. Let it go. That's right, I said you should let it go.

I personally don't feel you need to meet a man's family unless you're talking marriage. If it doesn't impact your life, leave it alone. This may sound cold, but I think it's smart. Everyone in his family, from his mom and dad to his brothers and sisters, will have an opinion about what they want for their little boy, and you may not fit the bill. Wait until you both fall in love and there's not a snowball's chance in hell his family can talk him out of you and into Betsy from next door.

If all goes well and you do decide to spend an eternity with your guy, you'll be happy you waited. A lifetime with him means a lifetime with the in-laws and that's not always a bed of roses. Enjoy the carefree, passion-filled dating stage and leave the heavy stuff for later.

FRIENDS

Meeting his friends is all together different. You want to do this as soon as possible. These are the people he chooses to spend his free time with, the ones he feels close to and comfortable enough with to let down his guard. These are the people who will help you get to know the real man behind the fake man.

Gain their trust and make them feel special and your guy will be putty in your hands. He wants his friends to like you and to look up to him for dating you. He doesn't want them to say, "Hey, man, she's a real bitch. What are you doing with her?" Avoid this at all costs.

You also don't want to try to become *their* best friend, too. That's his circle. You have yours and he has his—keep it that

---

NO DRIVE

Dear Jula,
I'm in love with a man who isn't driven by success and money. He's happy working a blue-collar job, making an average wage, and living a mediocre lifestyle. I'm not. Should I stay with the man I love or go for someone with money, someone who can give me all the things I want in life and then some?
Sheila

Dear Sheila,
Follow your heart. If your heart is more into money and material things, then go for it. But if being in love is more important, embrace your man just the way he is and make your own money. This way you can have it all—love *and* money.
Jula Jane

---

way. You can have fun when you're all together but don't make plans with them on the side. He won't like it and neither would you if it were reversed. Furthermore, if you stop dating each other, it's easier for you to go back to your friends, and for him to go back to his without them having to pick sides. Keep it clean.

PLANS FOR THE FUTURE

You want a man with a plan. He needs to know where he's going and how he's going to get there. He needs to have a savings account with five dollars or five million dollars—it doesn't matter. He just needs to have one. It shows fore-thought and planning. And he needs to have ambition. Without ambition he's doomed, and so are you.

Your man with a plan will know what he wants to do with his life. He'll know if marriage is for him, and whether he wants children or not and when. He'll know what he wants in a woman—and if that woman is you. He'll also know he wants a woman with a plan. Do you have a plan? You do, if you studied Chapter 2, "If You Build It, He Will Come."

So there you have it. Become a detective or a spy, which-ever you find sexier, and investigate your potential mate. It's okay to check out a man's package, so lose your fears and in-hibitions, and grope around until you find what you're looking for. And if you get caught, tell him I made you do it.

Chapter Quiz

When It Comes to a Man's Package, Does Size Really Matter?

1. When a man tells you he has a private jet you:
   A. Are genuinely impressed and brag to your girlfriends about the jet-set lifestyle you're going to have.
   B. Laugh out loud and ask him to put up or shut up—you've heard this one before.
   C. Smile sweetly and change the subject, knowing that most men who say this are lying. You realize that it will be better that you didn't make a big deal out of it if you end up in a relationship.

2. You have been dating a man for several months and begin to see contradictions in his stories. You:
   A. Keep it to yourself, look for the truth and then, armed with the real story, decide whether to stay and work it out—or to call him on it and leave.
   B. Call him a big fat liar and ask him never to speak to you again.
   C. Say nothing—the perks of being with him are too good to lose over a few not-so-white lies.

3. If a man has a long history of mental illness in his family you:
   A. Nickname him crazy and play with his emotions.
   B. Don't give it another thought until it affects your life.
   C. Ask yourself if this is something you can handle, since mental illness can be hereditary. If the answer is no, you let him down gently and move on. And if the answer is yes, you prepare yourself for a future with possible challenges in this area.

4. When you meet a man with no money in the bank and no career aspirations but a charming personality and a body that won't quit, you:
    A. Begin dating him and try to change him to better suit you.
    B. Take him on as a boy toy and look for a sugar daddy to foot the bill.
    C. Pass him up, knowing that you want more from life than he will ever be able to provide.

5. If you fall in love with a man you later learn isn't who he says he is you:
    A. Spiral down into a deep depression and wonder if you'll ever meet a man who won't lie to you. You decide the answer is no, so you stay with him.
    B. Take some time to decide if these are lies you can live with, or lies that will cause you to leave.
    C. Leave him immediately and never look back.

6. You want a man who is your equal, someone you can build a life with and trust, so you:
    A. Keep dating and keep searching until you find him. Then when you think you've found him, you do a background check on him.
    B. Only go out with men who fit your exact criteria.
    C. Compromise your needs because nobody seems to fit the bill and you're tired of being alone.

7. You believe men lie about who they are and what they have:
    A. Simply to get unsuspecting women into bed.
    B. Because they want to impress you and feel the need to create an elaborate persona to win you over.
    C. As a means of entertainment.

8. If the man you're dating doesn't have an exciting profile, but you really like him anyhow and want to continue seeing him you:
   A. Create a fictitious persona for him that you secretly share with friends and family and hope he never finds out.
   B. Talk yourself out of liking him and try to meet someone more intriguing.
   C. Continue to look at him with loving eyes because you don't allow what other people think influence your decisions about whom you date.

9. The man in your life is obsessed with sports—a fact you've known since day one. You thought it was cute when you first met but now you:
   A. Accept it as part of who he is and fill your free time with things that you enjoy.
   B. Resent it and want him to quit watching baseball and to go shopping with you instead.
   C. Get so turned off by his obsession, you feel yourself pulling away from him.

10. If you think your boyfriend is lying to you, you:
   A. Hack into his computer, credit card accounts and phone records to look for proof.
   B. Give him the benefit of the doubt and try to get to the truth in a legal and not too invasive way—and you keep your eyes wide open.
   C. Do nothing. All men lie.

Your Results

If you chose the following answers,
you know how to accurately size up a man's package:

1. **C.** You let a man pump up his own ego and never burst his bubble, an endearing quality.

2. **A.** An informed decision is so much better than a blind one, which is why you look for the facts and proceed with your best interests in mind.

3. **C.** Not one to kick a man while he's down, you handle challenging situations with finesse.

4. **C.** As tempting as a handsome man can be, you never waste your time—or his—on something that will never work. You want to remain available to meet a man more suitable for you.

5. **B.** You are no longer idealistic and make mature decisions, whether they hurt or not.

6. **A.** You don't fall for just anyone. You take chances and fall for just the right one.

7. **B.** You aren't cynical, you're realistic. This helps you to deal with the real world.

8. **C.** Keeping up with the Joneses isn't what you're all about. You're confident enough to be who you are, and allow him to be who he is.

9. **A.** You chose your man based on who he is—not on what you want him to be—and that frees you up to enjoy the life you chose.

10. **B.** You aren't one to be walked on and you're not one to overreact, either. You're a thorough fact checker who knows that timing is everything.

Chapter 8

It Might Be A Red Flag If . . .

Secret #8: Men Always Show You Who They Really Are

Behavior is the mirror in which everyone shows their image.
—Johann Wolfgang von Goethe

Dating is an investment in your future and should be treated with as much caution as you use when buying a stock or a condo, or anything else that costs time and/or money. You wouldn't fork over twenty grand (an amount you saved over four years, three weeks, six days and exactly five-and-a-half minutes) for a new stock just because it *seems* like a good choice. No, you'd study it inside and out before making that kind of commitment. You'd find out the five W's (the who, what, when, where, and why) *plus* the what ifs, wouldn't you?

CHEAP DATE

Dear Jula,
I just recently started dating a guy a few years younger than me. He's good-looking, treats me well and is a lot of fun, but I think he has a money problem or is just cheap. He's borrowed money from me on several occasions, to pay for parking (he didn't have cash on him), to pay for our entrance into a club (again, no cash), and once, to pay for our meal (he forgot his wallet). So far he hasn't paid me back. Is this a sign of what he's like or sheer coincidence?
Rebecca

Dear Rebecca,
This is a definite red flag. My best guess is that he's tight on money but still wants to date you and have a good time. He should be more upfront about his situation and tell you he can't afford to go out all the time, instead of taking money from you and making up lame excuses.
If you truly like him, save his ego and suggest activities that don't cost a lot, like a picnic in the park, or pizza and a movie at home. This way, you can still enjoy each other's company while taking it easy on his wallet, and yours.
Jula Jane

Nor would you buy a condo online based on a picture and a description. No, you'd hire a professional real estate agent to show you the property, advise you of your options and negotiate the best price and terms for you. You'd also hire an inspector to look for hidden defects and make sure everything was in working order. Next, you'd pay a law firm to conduct a title search to make sure there were no outstanding liens or encumbrances and then and only then, would you consider parting with your hard-earned money and committing to making this your home.

So why would you risk your time, your finances and your heart on a man you haven't researched? Hopefully, you wouldn't. If you meet a man you really like and want to pursue a relationship with him, then do run a background check. This can be done online for a small fee, or you can hire a private investigator to do it for you. This should be a common practice for every woman, no matter who the man is—whether a friend introduces you to him, or you meet him at a bar. Every man warrants a check under the hood, which, incidentally, you'd certainly do before buying a car. This investigative work can be your little secret. You don't have to tell him or anyone else, for that matter. If he finds out, oh well. He should be proud of you for being responsible and protecting yourself. If he gets upset, he probably has something to hide. Good thing you found out early in the game.

GOOGLE

We're in the Google age. We meet a man and immediately Google him. For the few of you who don't know what I'm talking about, Googling someone means you type his name into the search box at *www.google.com*, along with other distinguishing information, such as the city where he lives, the college he graduated from (or so he says), the company where he works (maybe he really is the CEO of Microsoft), and so on.

Nine times out of ten, you're going to get a hit on him right away, if not a phone listing then a mention in his college newspaper. Here are some easy steps to conducting a quick Google search on the man of interest:

1. Start with the obvious, his name. Include a middle initial, if you know it—John C. Doe

2. City of residence—Chicago

3. Place of business—Microsoft Chicago

4. Professional title—CEO

5. Type in any other information you have on him.

THE BRUSH-OFF

Dear Jula,
I've been seeing this guy for a few weeks and just began sleeping with him. The sex is great but the after-party is lacking. The minute he's finished, he rolls over, stretches and says, "I have an early meeting. Do you mind if we call it a night?" I know what that means—please leave. Is he afraid of commitment and moving too fast, or does he really have early-morning meetings every time?
Caroline

Dear Caroline,
I hate to be the bearer of bad news, but there are no early morning meetings standing in the way of you spending the night. He just wants to end the night right then and there and not have the intimacy of breakfast and chit-chat the next day.
It's up to you to let it go on this way, his way, or to make your feelings count. If it's important for you to bond after sex by sleeping over, then that's what you should have. Let him know in a non-confrontational manner, and if he isn't open to it, be prepared to move on to someone who is.
Jula Jane

In mere seconds, a picture of this man will be painted for you, but beware—what you see isn't necessarily what you get. Some listings may not be applicable to him. There are other John Does in the sea. The John Doe wanted for armed robbery in downtown Chicago may not be your John Doe, and the John Doe who has a six-figure tax lien against him just might be someone else's man. Let's hope so, anyhow. Then again, the John Doe with the wife and three kids could very well be your online Casanova. Lucky you.

BOND, JANE BOND

Now that you have this information, it's time to sort it out. Tax liens are fairly easy to decipher. Drive to the county clerk's office and request a copy of the tax lien. They usually charge a minimal fee, as little as $1, to copy the record. Every state and county is a little different, so call before you go, make sure you know the correct process.

Determining if the armed robber on the security video is your guy can be solved with a photograph. Contact the sheriff's department holding the warrant for his arrest, and e-mail or mail them a picture of your guy. If the mug shots match, I'd change my number and hide out until his arrest.

The wife and kids matter stings on a different level. Getting to the truth may take a bit more time and effort. You need to find the marriage certificate, which is usually filed in the county of residence at the time of marriage. He may live in Chicago now, but where did he live when he got married, that is, *if* he got married? This is where some skillful social engineering comes into play. You have to get the information out of people who know him without letting them know what you're up to, and without him finding out.

This is not an easy thing to do. People are generally suspicious and will naturally mention your inquiries to their friend, John Doe. Don't come right out with, "Was John ever married?" Instead, you should say, "I wish I could've seen John in his heyday. What was he like?" This will get them talking about the glory days, which may give you openings to probe further. "I didn't know John was the star quarterback in high school. He's so modest. What school did you guys go to?" Now you have a piece of information you didn't have before. It's unlikely he'll tell John you asked where they went to high school but very likely he'd tell him you asked if he ever had a wife.

I use this technique quite often to sort things out that don't quite add up. If your man tells you he was a soccer player in the Olympics and was on tour in Europe, but you don't believe him, ask his friends. "Did you ever travel abroad with John?" When they look at you like you're crazy and reveal that he's never been out of the country, you'll know the truth: An Olympic soccer player he's not, big fat liar he is. It's all in the way you ask the question. Take that secret to the bank.

JAIL BAIT

Dear Jula,
I went out on a date with a man who told me he was just released from prison. His crime—drug trafficking and car theft. He's handsome, confident and honest with me. Should I give him a chance, or call it a night?
Janice

Dear Janice,
My first reaction is to say, "Next!" Then again, everyone deserves a second chance. He's paid his debt to society. Is he working towards getting his life back on track? If you're attracted to him and enjoy his company, go ahead and grant him a few more dates. Just be cautious and listen to your intuition.
Jula Jane

WHAT IS A RED FLAG?

A red flag is an indicator that something is amiss. It can be revealed through a comment, such as "I never wear a condom," or through characteristics and behavior. Perpetual lying is red flag number one. Identifying red flags is easy. You hear them, you see them, and you feel them; they're ever so palpable. Dealing with them is an entirely different matter. Turning a blind eye is easier than facing them and, consequently, ending the relationship.

You see him standing there, his blue eyes gazing into your soul, his gorgeous frame taunting you. Somehow, you can't quite make out what's in his large, powerful hand. You squint your eyes, but the gigantic object is unrecognizable. You say, half-aloud, "What is it? Wait, it looks like he's waving. Oh no,

FIRST DATE RED FLAGS

1. He says "I love you" during the second course of your very first dinner. Check, please!

2. He's obsessed with doing the deed. Don't fool yourself. Of course, you're irresistible and the chemistry is undeniable. But no, this isn't the first time he's tried to have sex on the first date. This is business as usual.

3. He admits to being married and that he still lives with his wife, but he swears he's in the process of a divorce. Call me when it's final. On second thought, don't call me ever again.

4. He forgets his wallet. If he's this scattered on date one, just imagine what you have to look forward to.

5. He spends half the night in the bathroom. Can you say druggie? Next!

PERSONALITY RED FLAGS

1. He lies about small things (his age), big things (his marital status) and really big things (the fact that he runs a drug cartel).

2. He angers easily and is ready to fight at the drop of a hat.

3. He's jealous and controlling. He doesn't want anything or anyone coming between the two of you, including your family and friends. Especially your male friends whom he made you quit talking to after date two.

4. He's insecure. His insecurities are the foundation for your future unhappiness.

5. He's stubborn. His family didn't support him when he wanted to open a sandwich shop 14 years ago and he hasn't spoken to them since. You'd better not cross him.

BEHAVIORAL RED FLAGS

1. He doesn't make you a priority. People who truly love each other want to be together as much as possible. It's okay for you to want to see him.

2. He brings his own booze, hidden in a flask, into the restaurant and orders a Coke, and then mixes the two when no one's looking. If he's cheap with himself, he's going to be cheap with you.

3. He lives with his parents and makes no apologies about it. Why should he move out when he's got it so good? His mom makes his bed, washes his clothes, prepares his meals and cleans up after him. Guess whose job that will be next.

4. He won't get a paying job because he's too busy chasing his dream (he's a starving artist). He doesn't want to compromise his principles (he's lazy).

5. He answers his phone during sex. Need I say more?

hmm . . . he's waving *something*. It's red. Oh, this is exhausting. Why can't I see it? It's right there in front of me." The reason why you can't see it is because you're choosing not to.

We want to find love and to be in love so badly, we are willing to ignore obvious red flags for fear of losing that love. That's the sad but honest truth. We've all done it and some of us still do. Let's have some fun and laugh at ourselves for a minute. Below, you'll find several lists identifying red flags. Ask yourself the tough question: Is this something I would overlook or is it something that would make me walk away.

DEAL BREAKER RED FLAGS

1. He cheats on you. Once a cheater, always a cheater.

2. He hits you. Hit me with your best shot because it's the last thing you're going to do.

3. He steals from you. What's mine is yours; just ask first.

4. He's verbally abusive. This can be just as painful as physical abuse.

5. He's unkind to animals. Pick on someone your own size.

Keep in mind, a red flag is not conclusive evidence that someone wouldn't make a good mate. It's merely a sign that you need to investigate further before committing to a life with him *or* starting a life without him.

Gather intelligence, fact check and then give him an opportunity to come clean. If he refuses to give you a reasonable explanation or to even admit he's guilty—and you know without a shadow of a doubt he's lying—you may want to rethink the relationship. Sure, everyone deserves a second chance, but remember: Fool me once, shame on you; fool me twice, shame on me.

Chapter Quiz

Do You Recognize a Red Flag When You See One or Do You Turn a Blind Eye?

1. A man stands you up on three different occasions. You:
   A. Justify his behavior by thinking he's successful and very busy—it's not his fault.
   B. Quit taking his calls and never see him again.
   C. Get revenge by doing the same thing to him.

2. You Google someone you met in a bar and find out he's listed as a sexual offender. You:
   A. Blow it off thinking he must have a high sex drive and will be great in bed.
   B. Make up an excuse when he calls and try to avoid him as much as possible.
   C. Give him a chance to explain and then decide how to proceed.

3. If you spot a red flag you:
   A. Take note of it and watch for other warning signs.
   B. Ignore it. Facing it is so much harder.
   C. Analyze it with your girlfriends and let them tell you what to do.

4. When a man shows signs of hostility when speaking of an ex you:
   A. Get turned on by his hot-blooded temper.
   B. See it as a sign of what's to come if you happen to cross him.
   C. Try to calm him down and change the subject.

5. Hearing a man profusely praise his mother time and time again, and observing how he lets her make decisions for him, is:
   A. A clear red flag that his mother would be a huge part of your life if you end up with this guy.
   B. So cute and refreshing. More men should love their mommies like he does.
   C. A big fat turn-off. Grow up, Peter Pan.

6. When on a first date a man asks you to split the tab you:
   A. Oblige but think twice before going out with him again. You believe the person who initiated the date should pay the bill, and the fact that he didn't is a sign that he may be cheap or simply not your kind of guy.
   B. Whip out your black card and pick up the whole thing—just to make a fool out of him.
   C. Call him a cheapskate and refuse to pay.

7. On your fifth date with a man he tells you about his three small children whom he almost never sees. He assures you they won't interfere with your relationship. You find this:
   A. A breath of fresh air. Too many dads are hands on and frankly, you don't want his past getting in the way of your present.
   B. Not just a deal killer, but an absolute shame—for his children and their mother. You would have preferred it if he had said he has three children whom he loves and adores, and that he hopes to have more someday—with you.
   C. Irrelevant. What do his children have to do with you?

8. When a 40-year-old man is impressed that your last relationship lasted a year, then reveals that his record is three months, you:
   A. Take that red flag and politely run with it—as far away from him as possible. Unless, of course, you're just looking for a quick fling.
   B. Think he just hasn't found the right one yet and believe it will be different with you.
   C. Tell him how pathetic he is and ask him to never call you again.

9. If a man answers his phone during sex you:
   A. Wait for him to finish his call and without a word, let him pick up where he left off.
   B. Grab the phone out of his hands, push him off the bed and launch into a tirade about how big of a jerk he is.
   C. Say nothing. You simply get dressed, walk out and never sleep with him again.

10. A 35-year-old man addicted to PlayStation is a man to be:
    A. Avoided. He clearly hasn't matured and probably never will. In the long run, his childish ways will drive you insane, especially if you get stuck with all the chores while he's playing with his joystick.
    B. Cherished. You, too, are addicted and need someone to play with you.
    C. Ridiculed. You date him but make fun of his behavior, hoping your slights will make him change his ways.

Your Results

If you chose the following answers, then it's official—
you know a red flag when you see one and
aren't afraid to deal with it:

1. **B.** You're not the type of woman who allows herself to be taken for granted, nor are you someone who seeks revenge in order to make yourself feel better. You're a self-assured woman who knows her worth.

2. **C.** Knowing you can't always believe what you read, especially on the web, you give him an opportunity to tell his side of the story and then form an opinion and plan of action.

3. **A.** Red flags aren't meant to be ignored and they're not meant to push you into rash decisions. They're a sign of what may be in your future, which is why you pay attention to them and use them as a guide.

4. **B.** You never underestimate a man's temper, especially if he's shown you a glimpse of that side of him.

5. **A.** You aren't too keen on the idea of a man's mother controlling you or your man, so you move on when the momma's boy red flag gets waved.

6. **A.** You have principles and when those principles are challenged, you respond in a diplomatic manner.

7. **B.** You recognize that the way a man treats his own flesh and blood is a tell-tale sign of how he'll treat you.

8. **A.** A man who can't commit or who gets kicked to the curb in record time is not a man for you, so you don't waste your time on him.

9. **C.** A man who shows you so little respect doesn't deserve you; you know it and now, so does he.

10. **A.** Video games are for children and since you don't date children, you don't date Mr. PlayStation.

Chapter 9

The Purchase-Driven Life

Secret #9: You Can Have it All—If You Make it Happen

*There certainly are not so many men of large fortune in
the world as there are pretty women to deserve them.*
—Jane Austen

Gold diggers, unite! This chapter's for you. Someone once
said, "You can fall in love with a rich man as easily as a poor
man," and frankly, it's true.

TINKER WITH FATE

I believe we control our own destiny to a large degree and that nothing happens by chance alone. For example, you're not going to have a chance encounter with The Prince of Wales while sitting in your living room eating cookies. No, you have to make it happen. If you aspire to meet Prince William, then get off the sofa and get on a plane bound for London.

It's absolutely within your power to be in the right place at the right time. If you want to date a celebrity, go to L.A. If you want to date a billionaire, go to Forbes.com. And if you want to date a prince, get a publicist. You know he's out there; the problem is he doesn't know *you're* out there. So let him know. And do it sooner than later, before somebody else does.

Decide what tax bracket or social arena you want to play in and go for it. But remember—you're not the only one playing in this sandbox. There are thousands of women across the globe vying for the same man. What makes you so special? Go back to your *Great Woman* list in chapter 1 and read it, then decide if you have what it takes to win the heart of a celebrity, a billionaire, or even a prince. If the answer is no, then step up your game until the answer is yes. It's all up to you. Remember, if you build it, he will come.

DIGGING FOR GOLD

Dear Jula,
I've had a hard life and I'm tired of struggling. I think my way out is to marry a rich man. I'm an attractive blonde who normally dates hot young guys with no dough. It's getting me nowhere fast. I'm ready to land a rich man: young or old, fat and bald, I don't care. He just has to have money and be willing to spend it on me. How can I make this happen?

Katie

Dear Katie,
I understand where you're coming from but you need to relax. Your desperation is filling the air

BILLIONAIRE BOYS CLUB

So you want to date a billionaire, do you? So does every other gold-digger. According to the *Forbes's 2007* list of billionaires, there are 946 billionaires in the world, with a combined net worth totaling $3.5 trillion. And of course, some of these are married. Still interested?

First things first. You have to learn about the man you're targeting and the type of woman he's attracted to. This information is readily available at *www.forbes.com*. Or you can Google "billionaires" and surf away. Print out a complete list of billionaires. Highlight any man who interests you then do your research: Where is he from? What does he do? How much is he worth? Where does he play? Is he married? Does he have children? You get the picture. Get the scoop on him inside and out, backwards and forwards. Then take a long hard look at his face and ask yourself, "Is this a face I can wake up to every morning—a man I can kiss and make love to every night? Or even, "Will I be happy living in Kazakhstan?" If the answer is, "Yes, so long as I'm dripping in diamonds and drunk on champagne," you're good to go.

It's important to consider the following: Because a billionaire is a rare commodity (and knows it), he usually dates the world's most beautiful and glamorous women and celebrities. Don't get discouraged just yet. The fact of the matter is, you don't have to be beautiful or a celebrity to land a billionaire. Look at Melinda Gates. She's married to the richest man in the world, Bill Gates, and she's not a Hollywood star, nor is she a blonde bombshell. Her luck was a matter of being in the right place at the right time. Melinda was a manager at Microsoft for nine years, during which time she met, dated and married its founder. Now that's a raise I wouldn't turn down.

like a cheap perfume. You don't need to lower your standards just to find a rich man. There are a lot of good-looking men with hair on their heads who happen to have money.

Change your ways. No more broke hotties. Go to different places than you usually do so you can meet a whole new set of people. Join a new gym. Switch grocery stores and gas stations. What I'm telling you is to change things up and you will meet the man you're looking for. One more thing—hold out for someone you love. Don't just marry for money. It's an empty life.

Jula Jane

Many billionaires live and breathe their work, so they don't have time to get out and meet women outside of the office. They usually fall for someone right under their noses. It's true—several men on the *Forbes* list actually met their wives in the office. Next stop, human resources! Seriously, consider working for your dream man's company. This puts you one step closer to meeting him and sweeping him off his feet. Update your resumé and you're on your way to becoming a billionaire's wife.

WHEN THE RING'S NOT AN OBSTACLE

If the billionaire you have your heart set on is married, it's best to select someone else. Then again, if you'd be happy as his mistress, by all means, stalk away—but only if your conscience will allow it. Keep in mind that not all married men are morally untouchable. In some cultures, a man is allowed more than one wife. Feel free to become wife number 2, 3, or 4—it's allowed. But before you walk down that aisle, make sure you are completely informed about his country's customs and that you're comfortable with them.

STAR STRUCK

This is a completely different nut to crack. The celebrity male usually has an over-inflated ego and is used to getting whatever he wants, and surprise, surprise, he usually wants someone famous and hot. It's not often you see an A-lister with an

---

SHOPAHOLIC

Dear Jula,
I'm dating a great guy who buys me wonderful things: designer handbags and shoes, dresses and jewelry. I have it all but I want more. I covet things I know he can't afford—exotic cars, private jets, furs and couture. I know this is materialistic but that's me. I'm happy with my man but keep looking for his richer replacement. My friends call me shallow. Am I?
Stacey

Dear Stacey,
Shallow's a bit harsh. I'll agree you're materialistic. Luxury items bring you pleasure, just like a new set of clubs brings a golfer pleasure. He won't be condemned for his wants but you sure

average Jane on his arm. There are a few notable exceptions, however: Chris O'Donnell married his longtime girlfriend, Kindergarten teacher Caroline Fentress. (They have five, count 'em, *five* children.) And Matt Damon met his wife, Luciana Barroso, at a club where she was bartending.

So what's the typical girl to do? Become *not* so typical by becoming famous. Move out to Hollywood, get a job as a hostess at the hottest club and hope to be discovered. This may sound ridiculous but so is the desire to date a celebrity. You're digging for a needle in a haystack engulfed in flames, but if that's what you're determined to do, so be it.

How can you become hot and famous? Bleach your hair, buy some boobs, and run up and down the beach, it worked for Pamela Anderson. Maybe it'll work for you too. Or you can use similar tactics as with the search for a billionaire. Locate, research, and stalk. If you want to date a celebrity, you have to get in his way. Cross his path. Make him notice you. I think the *Enquirer* is hiring paparazzi. Say cheese.

PRINCE CHARMING

Every little girl dreams of marrying her Prince Charming one day. You can make that dream come true if you really strive for it. Look at Grace Kelly before she became Grace, Princess of Monaco, and Diana Spencer, who became Diana, Princess of Wales. I bet they, too, dreamed of marrying Prince Charming, but did they think he would be an actual prince?

Meeting, dating and marrying a real prince may not be easy, but it is feasible. You must act the part. Study the images of queens and princesses around the world and take note of their mannerisms, and how they behave and what they say. You must become one of them to walk among them.

Royalty must be selective in who they date, so clean up your act (and your rap sheet) before you set sail for the royal aisles. Use proper grammar when speaking, and for God's sake, enunciate. Your Southern drawl may have been cute when you accepted your Ms. Cherry Blossom award, but it won't seem so cute when you're curtseying before the Queen Mum. Practice your speech over and over until you neutralize your accent. You'll be perceived to be of higher intelligence and character if you speak with a fluid tongue.

Change your image. Become *Town and Country*—literally. The upper crust wear their thick waves of hair in neat ponytails and buns, or pulled back with a headband, and so should you. They never sport extensions streaked with brown and gold down to their backsides, and neither should you. Their nails are perfectly-manicured, with pale pink and clear polish—never black. And their attire is always occasion appropriate: slacks and a collar shirt for golf; riding pants and a jacket for the ponies; a ruffled skirt and sweater set for dinner. Think classic and preppy.

Changing your image is just the beginning of the battle. You still have a lot of work to do. You have to change your lifestyle. This means no more late nights spent doing shots and drinking beer at the pub; now you must immerse yourself in activities that attract the caliber of man you want. You'll want to attend art gallery openings, fashion shows, wine tastings, charity auctions and horse races. Play where *he* plays and in time, he will notice you. Oh, and don't forget—locate, research and stalk. You must do your homework if you hope to meet a prince, and you must also be dedicated and diligent in your efforts to win his heart. With a lot of change and a lot of hard work, it can be done.

REALITY CHECK

Dreaming big is always fun and I highly encourage you to always set your sights high, but sometimes a little reality check is in order. The odds of you actually meeting and marrying, or even just dating, a celebrity, a billionaire, or an actual prince, is highly unlikely. I'm not saying this to discourage you; I just want you to be realistic in your dating endeavors.

Your ultimate goal should be to meet a man who is like-minded, ambitious, giving and fun to be with. He should motivate you to be a better person and to follow your heart. This man may or may not have a lot of money, but this shouldn't be all that important if he's everything else that you want him to be. I promise you, money doesn't buy happiness—it buys *things*.

MILLIONAIRE WANTED

Okay, okay, I get it. You still want a man with lots of dough. It's not my place to judge you; I'm here to educate you, so here goes. There are plenty of millionaires in the world—some young, some old, some fat, some thin. Basically, they come in all shapes and sizes. But you probably don't care about those things; you just want to know how much he's worth and where and how to meet him.

It's fairly easy. They're all around you: at the grocery store, at the gas station, on an airplane sitting next to you, sipping a cocktail at your local bar. The trick is to determine who the real millionaires are in a sea of posers. Every man you meet is

EN-TITLED

Dear Jula,
I want to be a princess. Don't laugh; I'm being serious. I want a title. Princess is my first choice but I'd settle for Duchess or Countess. I'm still young and have my looks. I don't come from much but I've spent my whole life preparing to become royalty. I can walk the walk and talk the talk. I just need someone to walk with and talk to. Help.
  Princess Wannabe

Dear Princess Wannabe,
I'm not going to burst your bubble because I think it's fantastic when people dream big. If a title is that important to you, buy it. Find a destitute royal in some European country and offer to pay him to adopt you. Presto, you have a title.
  Jula Jane

going to tell you he's a millionaire, whether he is or not. He can't help it, it's in his genes. He wants to impress you and get you into bed, and what better way to do that than to dangle his money in front of your nose. It's worked a hundred times before and it will work again and again, if you let it. Here are some tell-tale signs to watch out for:

1. If he says he's a millionaire, he's probably not. Most men of wealth don't feel the need to flaunt it, unless they're insecure. Only then will they talk about money and material things incessantly, believing it's the only way to get a date with you. And maybe it is.

2. If he says he has a jet, he's lying. Only one in one million men who tell you they own a plane will actually be telling the truth. The only way to find out for sure is to fly in it. "I'd love to take you on my jet, Sweetie, but unfortunately, it's in the shop." Yeah, right, and my other car is a Bentley.

3. If he talks about his houses in St. Tropez, Dubai and New York, but invites you back to his apartment, he's not a millionaire. He's a poser. He'll have a great reason for why he's living in an apartment: he hasn't found the right house yet, he's not staying in the city, or, my personal favorite, his house is being remodeled. Don't believe him. Ask to see pictures of his other homes. If he can't produce them or he shows you pictures of "his house" in an article in *Architectural Digest,* he's lying.

4. If your guy lets you pay every other time, he's not a millionaire, or he's cheap—and you don't want him anyway. A millionaire will always pick up the tab. He's used to doing so and he enjoys doing so.

The signs are there. You just have to know what you're looking for and not let your eagerness for money take control. A rich man usually wears an expensive watch. It's a rite of passage and often the first thing he buys when he comes into money. If the guy chatting you up at the bar is sporting a Swatch but claims to be a CEO, he's lying. Don't be fooled by men who buy expensive bottles of champagne and tip heavily, either. Any guy with a credit card can do this. In fact, a lot of men with modest incomes spend lavishly at restaurants to pick up pretty girls because they know it works. This is Dating101 in the man's guide to getting laid. Wine and dine equals sixty . . . Well, you know the rest.

Here's the deal. The only way you're going to truly know if a man is a millionaire is to 1) Get a copy of his most recent bank statements, investment accounts and tax return; 2) Spend time with him and check out his houses, cars, planes, jewelry, shopping habits, bill-paying capabilities (yours!), etc., yourself; 3) Ask his mother. You simply can't take his word for it.

FOR LOVE OR MONEY

This chapter is titled *The Purchase-Driven Life* for a reason. It's speaking to those who seek wealth and all the pretty little things that money can buy. This is what you've deemed important and this is what you want to attain. But what about love? Are you willing to sacrifice love for money?

There are two schools of thought. One is that love fades so you might as well go for the money, and the other holds that money doesn't buy you happiness, so you might as well go for love. You can argue both of these points endlessly, depending on your personal views. Yes, love fades—not always, but quite often. And no, money doesn't buy you happiness but it does make life a lot easier. I say go for both love and money. Don't marry or even date for money. Hold out for someone you love who happens to be rich. Cha-*ching!*

Chapter Quiz

Are You A Gold-Digger or Are you Willing to Work for What You Want in Life?

1. If a man has a lot of money and is willing to spend it on you, you:
   A. Date him despite his wicked disposition and terrible breath. After all, money does buy happiness and breath mints.
   B. Count your lucky stars because the bank is about to foreclose on your house and you're all out of cash and options.
   C. Let him, but only if you truly adore him and can return the favor by cooking fabulous dinners for him and providing much-wanted companionship.

2. You believe work is:
   A. For unattractive women with no other options.
   B. Something you do to attain the material things you desire, a means of paying your bills and an invaluable way to maintain your independence—no matter what your circumstances are.
   C. The most important thing in a man's life, so you will play second fiddle to his job because that's how he gets the money he spends on you.

3. The idea of dating a celebrity is:
   A. A fun fantasy, but not something you focus your efforts on. There are more attainable fish in the sea.
   B. The key to your happiness. Since you don't have fame on your own, you seek it through dating a celebrity.
   C. Overwhelming. You can't imagine having to deal with other women throwing themselves at your man because you're afraid of what his reaction would be.

4. You want a lavish lifestyle so you:
   A. Work hard and continue your formal education as a means of making enough money to buy the things you covet so much.
   B. Latch on to a dying old man who happens to be rich, in hopes of scoring a place in his will.
   C. Date several men who contribute to your luxury fund.

5. You believe you deserve a successful man because:
   A. You're pretty and willing to do anything he wants in return for security.
   B. You're a successful woman and want an equal to complement your life.
   C. Anything less wouldn't be good enough to measure up to your friends' husbands and boyfriends.

6. When you meet a woman who appears to have it all—a big house, a fancy car, designer clothes and enough jewelry to rival Elizabeth Taylor—you:
   A. Immediately assume she's a kept woman and resent her for it.
   B. Try to become her friend so you can ride her coattails and expense account.
   C. Are happy for her and don't give it another thought.

7. Your best friend is dating a billionaire, not because she likes him, but because she likes his money. You:
   A. Act loyal and supportive to her face and hit on him behind her back.
   B. Try to talk some sense into her on a daily basis because you'd rather see her with a man she loves, instead.
   C. Are a true friend so you share your opinion with her when she asks for it and you give her your respect, but not necessarily your approval.

8. If a man you've been dating loses his wealth you:
    A. Stand by him and help him rebuild his fortune any way you can.
    B. Dump him for a rich man who can keep you in the lifestyle you've grown accustomed to.
    C. Stay with him but get a sugar daddy on the side.

9. Your rich boyfriend helps you start and grow your own company. Once you achieve great success you:
    A. Toss him aside. You can support yourself now and want a younger, hotter man, instead.
    B. Do something special for him to show your gratitude.
    C. Give him all the credit and majority ownership out of a sense of obligation.

10. If you had to choose between love and money you would:
    A. Wholeheartedly choose love, even if that meant you had to live in poverty.
    B. Give up the love of your life for a man with money.
    C. Hold out for both—why settle when you can have it all?

Your Results

If you chose the following answers, you're not a gold-digger, you're an ambitious woman:

1. **C.** You don't see a problem with a man lavishing you with gifts, so long as you genuinely like him and find a way to show your appreciation.

2. **B.** You're a wise woman who knows the importance of being self-sufficient.

3. **A.** Your expectations are realistic and will allow you to find a quality man sooner than never.

4. **A.** There's no greater reward than living well on your own accord.

5. **B.** A quality woman never settles for less than she deserves, which is why you strive for greatness in your own life.

6. **C.** You're too busy enjoying your fabulous life to be jealous of someone else's.

7. **C.** You recognize that you don't have to agree with a friend's choices in order to be her friend, and this makes you a good friend to have.

8. **A.** You aren't the type of woman to let your man's misfortune ruin an otherwise great relationship. You push up your sleeves and help him regain what he lost and obtain even more.

9. **B.** You appreciate any help you're given and always give back in return—within reason.

10. **C.** You know you can have it all if you work hard and never give up on your dreams.

Chapter 10

Match.con

**Secret #10: Explore All Dating Options,
but Proceed with Caution**

*Any guy can sweep any girl off her feet;
he just needs the right broom.*
—Date Doctor, Hitch

A significant number of successful relationships and marriages have resulted from people meeting online, so why is there still such a stigma associated with connecting in cyberspace? So many profiles start with, "I can't believe I'm doing this." These same people fear their friends and coworkers will see them on-line. Guess what—if they see your profile, they're online, too.

Cyber dating is really quite useful and shouldn't be ruled out because of possible embarrassment. Think of the upsides. You get to meet like-minded people from all over the world who are looking for love. It enables you to date outside your local pool of men, and rule out men who dated women you know; married men; men with girlfriends; men who still live at home, men in your past; and, this should go without saying, men who are related to you.

THE WILD, WILD, WEST

I think the real challenge with online dating is the overwhelming amount of bull that's posted. When we go to a bar we expect men to feed us lines, but when we visit a professional dating site that supposedly screens its members, we're shocked and appalled when we find out the man we fell in love with is actually married with children. The best medicine for this ailment is to assume everyone is lying to some degree. Does that sound cynical? Maybe it is, but being aware and prepared is better than getting stabbed in the heart.

And if you can't beat 'em, you might as well join 'em. It seems as though women have followed in men's footsteps, paving a path of deception on their way to self-gratification. I don't condone it, but I don't blame them for it, either. Fair is fair gentlemen. Deal with it.

OH WHAT A TANGLED WEB WE WEAVE...

I've always wondered why men are so prone to lying when they meet a woman. For the most part, women don't lie about who they are or what they have. You don't hear a chick droning on about her sports car and big bank account, or her position as CEO of a major company. No, we talk about shopping and pedicures.

Actually, I've finally figured it out. Women don't lie about those things because we don't have to. Men don't care what kind of car we drive. In fact, they hope our car doesn't outshine theirs. And they don't care if we have lots of cash and big careers. No, they want us to have just enough dough to pay our own bills but not enough to afford life without them. Men want us to have something we can't lie about—good looks. They're either there or they're not. End of story. Or is it?

The launch of online dating opened up a new realm of possibilities. You can now pretend to be something you're not, like a size 2. Let's be honest, the picture you posted of yourself looking slim and trim in that sexy bikini may not be the most up-to-date representation of your wonderful self 25 pounds and three hairstyles later today. Who do you think you're kidding? That's just as bad as a man in a bar boasting about his private jet. At some point, the jig is going to be up and then what are you going to do?

Frankly, I don't have a reasonable answer, unless you never plan to meet a cyber mate face to face. If it's merely your fantasy world, then no harm, no foul. Well, that's not exactly true, is it? Is it fair to carry on seven weeks of online banter with a man who thinks he's talking to size 2? No, it's not. Or is it reasonable to think he's going to be so crazy about you from your online interaction that your size won't even matter? I don't think so.

I'm not picking on women over a size 2; I'm one of them. I'm simply trying to make a point. Men in bars lie because they can, while women in bars don't lie because they can't. A 200-pound woman can't say she's a size 2. A man won't believe her. But any man can say he has a private jet and get away with it, if only temporarily.

Oh what a tangled web we weave when we practice to deceive. It's true. Lies beget lies and before you know it, you've changed your primary residence to Fantasy Island. Here are the five most common lies told online. Be on the lookout:

1. "I'm single." (Nope, he's married.)

2. "You're the only one I'm corresponding with." (Not counting Sheila, Beth and Sue.)

3. "I don't usually date online." (Actually, I'm on six sites and have been for ten years. It gets me laid.)

4. "I'm good-looking and stupid rich, which is why I can't post my picture and full profile. Too many women would respond and I want to be selective." (I look like a toad and have $24 in my checking account.)

5. "I really want to meet you, but something came up and I won't be able to make it—again." (My wife got back into town early so I can't get away.)

also hurting other women with his lies. I don't know your personal situation so I urge you to proceed with caution. Before you confront him, print copies of his profile and activities online. He'll probably delete them and try to deny it.

Hear what he has to say and decide whether you're going to give him another chance. If so, I highly recommend counseling. You're going to feel betrayed and resentful, and don't even get me started on the trust issues that are going to plague you.

Make therapy a condition of staying together. It's important to get to the root of the problem in order to fix it and keep history from repeating itself.

Jula Jane

So you've fallen for a man you met online but something seems amiss. You can go with the flow and wait for the other shoe to drop, or you can be proactive and remove his shoe for him. It's easier than you think.

The top complaint I hear from women dating online is that the guy always promises to meet her face to face, but never shows up. He cancels with one lame excuse after the other. Here's what you do—you bait him. Create a profile that matches his geographically, physically and sexually. Post the bait and wait for him to bite.

Be considerate and throw back the other fish, meaning if it's not him, let him go. You're not doing this to meet men by pretending to be someone you're not. That won't get you anywhere. You're doing this to catch a liar red-handed so you can get over him and move on.

When your Mr. Wonderful finally contacts your cyber alter-ego, you'll be able to find out if his excuses have merit. Remember, the cyber space you is everything he says he wants in a woman, so use that to draw him out. Banter back and forth for a while. Ask all the questions you believe he's given you false answers to, and then ask to meet him in person. If he obliges and follows through with it, you'll know he's been leading you on with no real intention of starting a relationship. After all, how does he have time for her, a woman he just met, but not for you, a woman he's been talking to for six months? When he finds out what you've done, your online gigolo may lash out. The best thing to do is keep your discovery to yourself and simply move on. He doesn't deserve an explanation.

CON GAMES

It's a bit disenchanting to think so many people are lying. How are you ever going to meet a good, honest man when you're lying and he's lying, too? The answer is you're not. A healthy relationship is built on trust and honesty, so be who you are, no matter how tempting it is to be someone you're not. Just don't lose hope. There's a suitable man out there for you and you just might meet him online. But no matter where he is, it's up to you to find him. Just be prepared to weed through a lot of crap first.

The Office of Fair Trading (OFT) says dating frauds are becoming more common. A con artist will create an extremely attractive profile and post a photo of a great-looking person, who's not him. Then he'll target needy, lonely women, and plain Janes. Once contact is made with a potential victim and their trust has been gained, the con artist makes a move to obtain money or favors.

Don't assume you're exempted from his target group. You may not be needy or lonely, or even a plain Jane, but there's still a chance he'll pick you and you'll fall for his con. Watch for these tell-tale signs indicating a man is bogus and is trying to con you:

CON GAME

Dear Jula,
I'm corresponding with a beautiful woman online and think I'm falling in love with her. She's everything I've always wanted in a woman with one exception— she lives in another country. I've asked her to visit many times but she always tells me she can't take time-off from work, or that she can't afford a plane ticket. I offered to pay her airfare, but she still won't come, unless I send her cash to pay her bills while she's away. My friends tell me I'm an idiot if I send her the money, but I disagree. What do you think?
Donald

Dear Donald,
This sounds all too familiar. It's a common

scam for women to bond with a male online and then ask for cash. Here are a few things you can do to see if she's legit. Ask for her phone number and a home address where you can send the ticket. Also ask for a bank routing number to send the cash. If she won't give you this information and just wants cash wired anonymously, she may be conning you.

On the other hand, she may just be cautious. After all, she doesn't know you that well. Find out where she works and call her there. The more research you do, the better. If everything adds up, I don't see a problem with you helping someone you love, especially if you benefit as well—a face-to-face meeting.

Jula Jane

1. He resides in another city or country and tells you he wants to meet face to face but can't because he can't afford a plane ticket. He hopes you'll offer to buy him one and if you don't, he asks you to. If this happens, there's no doubt about it, you're being scammed.

2. He's only accessible via the Internet. If he doesn't have a phone number, he doesn't warrant further contact.

3. He asks you to call him at a 900 number and later you receive a phone bill for hundreds of dollars. Here's a tip: 1–900 equals dial for money.

4. His picture online is gorgeous and enticing, but his profile is vague and could fit almost anyone. This is a sign that he doesn't want his true identity known. He may be married or he may be trying to scam you and doesn't want you to be able to find him when he eventually gets caught.

5. If he talks about being a millionaire, he's not. This is a way to lure you so later he can convince you that his money is tied up in investments. He will say that he needs your help to secure his next big deal. Before you know it, he's cleaned out your savings account.

The best way to avoid online dating scams is to never give out personal information, such as bank account numbers and your address. Never, ever send money, and if something sounds too good to be true, it probably is. Listen to your intuition, no matter how handsome and convincing a man is, and you'll be fine.

WILL DATE FOR FOOD

As I was writing this chapter, I stepped out for a much-needed spa pedicure and, being the workaholic that I am, I interviewed everyone around me about their online dating experiences. No one admitted to having tried it themselves (yeah, right!), but each woman I talked to had a story to tell about a so-called friend who had.

The most interesting story concerned a college girl with very little money who used online dating as a way to get a free meal, literally. She was a cute girl determined to get an education and make a life for herself, but in spite of all her hard work, she was barely making it. Sometimes food had to take a back seat to more pressing issues, like rent and tuition. One day she decided to try online dating in hopes of landing dinner dates. It worked.

In no time at all, she was being wined and dined and just having a ball. One day she'd chow down on hot dogs and pretzels at a ball game, and the next day she'd enjoy a steak and lobster dinner, thanks to the older gentleman who thought she was simply adorable. There's nothing wrong with this, unless she was going out with guys she wouldn't normally date, or leading men

CLOSET CYBER DATER

Dear Jula,
I met my friends for happy hour one night and was absolutely humiliated by a total stranger. He recognized me from my online dating profile and walked up to me like he knew me. Before I could stop him, he was revealing things about me that I didn't want anyone in my circle to know, namely that I'm using an online dating service. He finished his rant and went about his day, leaving me to face the snickering faces of my friends.

I made up the lame excuse that he must have mistaken me for someone else, and denied ever dating online. I went home and immediately took my profile down, hoping no one would ever know it was really me. I'm disappointed, though. I had just started using an online dating service to meet men and it was going really well. Now, it's over. What do I do now?

Christy

on with no intention of having a real relationship. There has to be a win-win for it to be fair.

Everyone's looking for something when they join a dating service and that certain something varies, from true love to casual sex to, well, a hamburger. Therefore, it's important to find out what a man's intention is before you go too far. Here are some common reasons why people date online:

1. Looking for love: long-lasting, heart-warming, soul mate kind of love.

2. Looking to score: one-night stands, wham, bam, thank you ma'am.

3. Looking for a casual date, for a special occasion or any occasion, just nothing serious.

4. Looking to build an ego: already taken but needs a little "innocent" flirting to feel good.

5. Looking for companionship: in need of a friend or two (or three or four).

> Dear Christy,
> You should brush yourself off and get back on that dating site and continue your healthy, proactive quest for a perfect match. There's no shame in it. As for your friends, don't let their opinions get you down. So they made fun of online dating, so what? Ask them why online dating is bad but meeting random blokes in a bar is okay.
>
> I bet they would all like to try their chances online, but fear embarrassment, just as you do. Be the stronger girl in the group. Set the standard and watch them follow your lead. If not, they'll be eating their hearts out while you're on great dates every week and they sit on a bar stool waiting for Mr. Right to come along.
> Jula Jane

SAFETY TIPS

Dating is risky business, whether you meet a man in a bar, at a coffee house, at church, through friends, or online. The rules change a bit, though, when you date online because you haven't looked into his eyes and into his soul. Here are some tips that will help keep you safe and aware.

Match.con

Take it slow

Start out by corresponding solely via your dating service's internal e-mail. Look for odd behavior or inconsistencies. The person you're chatting with may not be who or what he says. Trust your instincts and if anything makes you uncomfortable, stop all communication immediately and indefinitely.

Remain anonymous

Never include your last name, home address, phone number, e-mail address, place of work or any other identifying information in your profile or initial e-mails. Stop communicating with men who pressure you for personal information, or try to trick you into revealing it.

May I see some I.D.?

Ask to see a photo. If he can't produce one he may be hiding something. A picture is worth a thousand words and will help you determine if this is someone you'd like to date. Keep in mind that the picture he sends you may not be of him.

Phone Skills

When you're completely comfortable you may exchange phone numbers with your online match, but only give him your cellphone number. When you call him, block your number by dialing *67, or whatever method your local phone company utilizes. Get to know him on the phone before meeting face to face. You'll learn a lot about this man from his phone skills.

LOST ONLINE

Dear Jula,
I'm 39 and have never been married. I don't have kids and I haven't been in a committed relationship in seven years. I date online exclusively but not successfully. When I meet someone I'm not interested in, I lie and say I have a boyfriend.

I do think I like this one guy, Dave. I met him online about six months ago. We talk on and off, actually more off than on. His excuse for not communicating more often is that he thinks he's going to fall too hard and I may not like what I see. He lives in another state and has backed out of visiting me three times. He's not married but has a seven-year-old who is the center of his world. He makes lots of promises yet he's never followed through on a single one. How do I let him know I'm interested in him and want more than just random contact, without scaring him away or seeming too desperate?

Justine

In Person

Once you've gathered enough information about your online date, you may arrange an in-person meeting. Do so on your terms. If you get cold feet at the last minute, cancel. You shouldn't feel obligated, no matter how close you've become. Trust yourself and trust your instincts.

Your Place or Mine?

When meeting off-line, you call the shots. Name the time and place of your choice and meet him there on your own accord. Never allow your date to pick you up at home. Tell a friend where you're going and whom you're meeting. Give her his name and phone number. In return, show her the courtesy of letting her know when you return home safely.

Date Protocol

Limit yourself to no more than one glass of wine or cocktail. You don't want to impair your judgment. If you change venues, take your own car. Insist upon it and don't allow him to ride with you. End the date with a thank you and a good night. Don't go home with him and don't invite him to come home with you.

Out of Town

When you travel to a different city to meet an online match, always make your own arrangements. Don't tell him where you're staying or when you're arriving. Make plans to meet him at a restaurant of your choice. Ask the concierge at your hotel for a suggestion. Drive yourself in a rental car, or better yet, arrange for the hotel car to drive you and wait for you. Do not allow your date to pick you up or drive you back. Tell a friend where you're going, who you're meeting, and when you'll be back. Stay in touch with your friend while you're away to let them know you're okay.

Word of Caution
Don't let your desire for a man get in the way of common sense. If you feel you're being lied to, if you feel you're in danger, or if you feel something just isn't right, you're probably right. Don't worry about looking foolish in his eyes—end the date. Your safety is more important than his opinion of you.

IT MIGHT BE A RED FLAG IF . . .

➤ He refuses to speak to you on the phone after connecting online for a significant period of time.

➤ He doesn't answer direct questions with direct answers.

➤ He shows signs of anger, acts in a passive-aggressive manner, or tries to pressure you.

➤ He makes demeaning or disrespectful comments, or comes on too strong.

➤ He lies about his age, marital status, profession, education, or any other personal detail.

➤ He looks or acts significantly different from his online profile.

WRAPPING IT UP

The bottom line: Cyber dating is merely another outlet for meeting men. There are risks and unknowns, so you should proceed with caution. Be smart, be aware, and have some fun.

Chapter Quiz

When It Comes to Online Dating, Do You Get Duped or Are You a Master Dater?

1. You are newly single and ready to date so you:
   A. Become an active member with several online dating sites as a way to meet eligible men.
   B. Sit at home and wait for friends and family to introduce you to potential suitors.
   C. Go out with your girlfriends on a regular basis but are too shy to talk to men.

2. Your online profile is:
   A. A combination of fact and fiction featuring a photo from your senior year in college—ten years ago.
   B. Witty, appealing and completely accurate.
   C. Vague. You're afraid your friends will make fun of you if they find out you're dating online.

3. If a man you've been corresponding with online repeatedly cancels plans to finally meet face to face you:
   A. Delete him from your inbox and from your heart, and move on to a man with follow through.
   B. Continue to give him chances, no matter how many times he lets you down, hoping that one day he will come through.
   C. Launch an online smear campaign against him until he agrees to meet you for coffee.

4. When you find out that someone you know is dating online you:

   A. Laugh at them to their face and behind their back, despite the fact you've tried it yourself.
   B. Feel sorry for them because they have to stoop so low to get a date.
   C. Say nothing unless they bring it up. Then you're supportive and genuinely curious about how well it's working for them.

5. You've stretched the truth a bit when corresponding online because:

   A. You feel you have to appear more exciting and more attractive than you think you naturally are in order to compete with other women.
   B. You accidentally pressed the wrong key when typing in your weight. (I meant I weigh 130 pounds, not 120 pounds—my bad.) Otherwise, you would never intentionally portray yourself as anything other than your fabulous self.
   C. It's a fun and easy way to inflate your ego and besides, they'll never know so no harm, no foul.

6. If a man is pressuring you to give him more personal information than you're comfortable with you:

   A. Tell him once more that you're not ready to divulge that information, and if he still persists, you drop him.
   B. Give in. What's the harm if he has your date of birth and social security number?
   C. Give him false data and continue the relationship until he finds out.

7. The fact that many studies state that one-third of the men online are married:

   A. Makes no difference to you. That's his wife's problem, not yours.
   B. Keeps you from dating online—what's the point?
   C. Explains why you are so cautious when chatting with a new match.

8. You're ready to meet an online match face-to-face:

   A. After the first wink. There's no time like the present.

   B. Once you've established a good rapport, have spoken on the phone and feel confident that what he says—and types—is true.

   C. After chatting consistently with him for a minimum of six months, and you've conducted a full background check and gotten a sample of his DNA—just in case you turn up missing.

9. You've had some bad experiences when trying to date on-line so you:

   A. Hang up your keyboard and hit the bars.

   B. Cry yourself to sleep every night and lose hope of ever meeting a man.

   C. Try, try again thinking you'll have better luck next time.

10. You agree to have a drink with someone you met online. You:

   A. Choose a restaurant where you know the staff and ask your date to meet you there. And just to be extra careful, you let your best friend know where you're going and who you're meeting.

   B. Tell him to pick you up at your house and invite him in when he arrives, hoping to impress him with your tidiness and hospitality.

   C. Get cold feet and stand him up at the last minute.

Your Results

If you chose the following answers,
then you are, without a doubt, a master dater:

1. **A.** You are proactive when it comes to dating and meeting men, which means you'll meet them sooner than later.

2. **B.** You are confident in who you are and don't feel the need to pretend to be something loftier.

3. **A.** You're not a woman who puts up with empty promises and disrespect, and in turn, you get the respect you deserve.

4. **C.** Being a sensitive sort, you don't mettle unless invited, and then you offer constructive words and advice—never harsh judgments.

5. **B.** Why stretch the truth when the truth is this attractive?

6. **A.** Your momma didn't raise no fool—the chances of you falling for an online con are slim to none.

7. **C.** You check the facts and check them again before you believe what you're told, especially online.

8. **B.** You like to take your time and not rush into new relationships, believing all good things come to those who wait.

9. **C.** A little bump in the road is not enough to deter you. You are determined and driven, and with qualities like these, you will succeed.

10. **A.** It's better to be safe than sorry—your tried and true motto.

Chapter 11

Pick Your No's

Secret #11: Don't Put Up with BS

When a man goes on a date he wonders if he's going to get lucky.
A Woman already knows.
—Frederick Ryder

So many men, so little time and though you'd like to say yes to all of them, you simply have to pick your no's from time to time. It's a dirty job, but somebody has to do it. But why oh why must you pick your no's, even when you don't want to? You'll get stopped up with man congestion if you don't. You need to clear the path for the right guy.

Let's analyze the different types of men in the dating pool and determine if they warrant a yes or a no.

YOUNG STUD

Ah yes, the young stud. He's barely legal, chiseled to perfection and has the stamina of the energizer bunny. He has big strong arms that wrap around you as he playfully lifts you into the air and tosses you into bed. Yippee! This is fun. He makes you feel like a school girl again, a naughty school girl at that. Who in their right mind would say no to him?

At first, no one, but in time his hotness takes a back seat to his undesirable package. For instance, his living arrangements: an old house that he shares with three of his college buddies and an ex-girlfriend—not exactly the kind of place an accomplished woman should be shacked up in. And his car, a 1992 Honda Accord, is littered with McDonald's wrappers and empty beer cans. How gross. And of course, there's the PlayStation. Don't even get me started on the PlayStation!

The young stud is meant to be an occasional treat, a distraction from the daily grind. He's a necessary rite of passage for every woman in her thirties and forties. He's not to be confused with boyfriend material, and certainly not marriage material. When it comes to the young stud, eventually, you must pick your no's.

PLAYER

The Player is, by far, one of the most frustrating types of men. He comes on strong in the beginning because he's in hot pursuit of what he wants—you. He's usually quite handsome and often, well-to-do, which makes him even more irresistible. You fall hard and you fall fast.

No longer able to resist his advances, you sleep with him and it's incredible. Afterwards, you curl up next to him and fantasize about your future together. That's right about the time he says, "Hey babe, I have an early morning meeting. I better take you back to your car." What? *Damn, I should have picked my no's.*

You just got traded down from the A team to the B team. This means he'll text you now and again to keep you interested, but his face time will be spent on a rookie—someone he hasn't gone to bat with yet. And just when you finally give up on him, he'll call you up and ask you out. Not for dinner, mind you. Those days are over. He'll ask you to come by his place to watch a movie, a.k.a. have sex. And he'll ask if you wouldn't mind picking up a pizza on your way over. Can you say "booty call"?

JEALOUS JOHN

The Jealous John wins your heart with his possessive behavior. He makes comments like, "You're so beautiful, every guy in here can't keep his eyes off you," or "I'm so crazy about you. Promise me you'll spend every free minute with me." These words are music to your ears, especially since you just ended a gut-wrenching affair with a player who had time for everyone but you. It's great for a while, then it becomes suffocating.

It turns out Jealous John isn't so much into you. He's just not into himself, meaning he can't be alone. He's incredibly insecure and needs you by his side at every waking moment, or he falls apart. What was once flattering is now overwhelming. If you find yourself consumed by a Jealous John—you're no longer hanging out with friends because it causes too much friction with him, or you're skipping family functions because he doesn't want to go and doesn't want you to go, either—it just might be time to dig down deep and pick your no's. Ah, see. Now you can breathe again.

GUY'S GUY

The Guy's Guy likes bars, boobs and baseball—and that's it. He can be found sitting on his favorite bar stool at the local pub, sipping a beer and tossing back shots on a dare. He's into big-breasted women, but only for sport—sport f***g, he calls it. The man loves his sports. Who can fault him for that? He knows the players' names and every stat in baseball, football, basketball, hockey, tennis, even golf, yet he can't seem to remember your first name or your birthday. Charming. "Hey Jill, I mean, Julie. Grab me a beer."

The Guy's Guy would much rather spend time with his buddies than with a woman. He's not gay, far from it. He just enjoys hanging with the guys much more than hanging with you. And don't think you can infiltrate his cave by becoming one of the guys. You can't. He doesn't want you high-five-ing him when his team scores and he doesn't want you burping the theme to *Rocky*. That's *his* job. He wants you for one thing only—sex. And when that's over, he wants you to go away so he can scratch himself and watch the game.

The Guy's Guy isn't a bad guy. He's just a bad guy to date, unless you're a Girl's Girl. And by that, I mean a woman who loves to shop, go to the spa with her best friend, spend time with her sisters, i.e. hang out with the girls—*all the time*. This particular kind of woman likes a man for two reasons—sex and

BROTHERS

Dear Jula,
I'm interested in a past boyfriend's brother and don't know what to do about it. I haven't dated my ex in over a year, but still feel like it might be wrong to date his brother. I usually have a strict policy when it comes to dating. I don't go out with anyone who has dated my girlfriends or someone I know. Shouldn't those same rules apply the other way around? I don't want to cause a rift between two brothers, but I also don't want to pass up an opportunity to explore a potentially wonderful relationship. Please give me your opinion.
Barbara

Dear Barbara,
You're treading on dangerous ground

money. They're perfect for each other. As for the rest of us, let's pick our no's.

MARRIED MEN

There are so many types of married men. Type A still lives with his wife and children, and pretends to be happy. He makes up excuses like, "I have to work late," or "I'll be out of town on business for a few days," so he can play with his mistress. He justifies his actions with the age-old phrase, "I can't help it; I'm a guy." He lays his cards out on the table and tells you, "I'm never going to leave my wife. I enjoy sleeping with you but know that it's never going to go farther than that." How touching. Pick your no's.

Type B still lives with his wife but plans to leave her when the time is right (or so he would have you believe). Somehow, the time is never quite right. Her mom just died, her birthday's coming up, she stubbed her toe, or the biggest excuse—she'll take all of my money. Type B will string you along until you put too much pressure on him, then he'll leave you for another woman—not his wife, but another mistress. It looks like he picked your no's for you.

Type C no longer lives with his wife. They're separated. He may or may not tell you that he's still married, though. Details, details, details. He hasn't gone through with the divorce for many reasons. He reasons, why do today what you can put off until tomorrow. Type C is complicated and may or may not be worth your time. If he is honest with you and neither of you is in a rush to get married, he

here, but if you handle the situation with dignity and honesty, I think you may have a chance at succeeding without hurting feelings. You haven't dated the first brother in almost a year, which puts quite a bit of distance between the two of you. I don't know the people involved or their personalities, but I find being open and considerate disarms most people.

Call your ex and ask how he would feel if you dated his brother. Hopefully he'll give you his blessing and you'll be able to go on with your life guilt-free. If he voices a concern about it, talk to him and explain your feelings. Unless he still has feelings for you, it shouldn't be a problem. Remember to be open and compassionate.

Jula Jane

just might be worth a yes for now, and a no's picking later.

DON'T PICK YOUR NO'S

You've always been told not to pick your nose. Well I'm saying pick away. I want you to pick your *no's* in public, in private, anywhere, anytime. Picking your no's should become your favorite thing to do. And once you master the art of no's picking, you'll finally be free to smell the cologne of a great man.

MAKING SENSE OF IT ALL

Women tend to say yes when they should say no. They say yes to Young Studs, yes to Players, yes to Jealous Johns, yes to the Guy's Guy, and worst of all, yes to Married Men. We've all done it and we've all regretted it. And we've all done it again and again.

We know why we date the wrong men. We're lonely and want someone, *anyone* to fill the void. What we don't know is how to stop ourselves. Women who've been stood up without a call, a reason, or even an "I'm sorry" but still give the jerk another chance; women who catch their man cheating and forgive him, only to watch him do this again and again; and women who are ignored and taken for granted yet stick around to feel the pain of being treated second to everything . . . these are the women who need to pick their no's the most.

I chose the catch phrase "pick your no's" as a way to get through to you. I know you'll remember this chapter and these words of advice because of this silly little phrase. I want you to say no to Young Studs, no to Players, no to Jealous Johns, no to the Guy's Guy, and no to Married Men. It's time to say yes to someone *great!* But the only way you're ever going to say yes to a Great Man is to say no to all of the not-so-great men that cross your path.

> If the man in your life has a child with you simply to please you, he won't be the best father to that baby and might resent you for it later. Even though it's going to be painful, I suggest you move on from this relationship, so you'll be free to meet the man of your dreams—a man who can't wait to have a baby with you.
>
> Jula Jane

Chapter Quiz

Do You Know When to Hold 'Em and When to Fold 'Em?

1. A boy toy is:
    A. Someone you enjoy once in a great while, but not someone you allow yourself to fall in love with—you know it will only lead to disappointment.
    B. Hot, hot, hot and what you always go for.
    C. Disgusting. Older women should never date younger men.

2. You handle a player by:
    A. Playing right back—two can play this game.
    B. Hanging out with your girlfriends and running to his side when he snaps his fingers.
    C. Casually dating him and not taking it too seriously, leaving yourself open to other suitors and opportunities.

3. Jealous men make you:
    A. Feel suffocated, if it's too much, and flattered, if it's just enough.
    B. Timid and afraid of being your outgoing self, for fear of setting them off.
    C. Wild with excitement as they feed your ego with their bar brawls in your honor.

4. A man who prefers watching sports and hanging with the guys to spending time with you is:
    A. A jerk and stands little chance with you.
    B. Not someone you want to commit your life to, but he could be a fun person to date casually. He can be your spare.
    C. Normal and like most guys you meet. It's just par for the course.

5. Married men are:
   A. Off limits.
   B. Taboo and oh so sexy. I love being the other woman who gets the romance and gifts while his wife takes care of washing his clothes and feeding his kids.
   C. People, too, and deserve to have a little variety in their lives, if that's what they need.

6. If you see a man you're casually dating with another woman you:
   A. Make a big scene and vow never to see him again, but do anyway—he's really hot.
   B. Give him a sincere nod and a smile and walk the other way. He isn't doing anything wrong, plus your date is on his way in.
   C. Run away in tears and text him incessantly until he turns his phone off, then you show up on his doorstep to wait for him to come home.

7. All men:
   A. Are jerks and deserve to be hurt just as they have hurt you.
   B. Have good qualities somewhere deep down inside which is why you date all men all the time—even men who are disrespectful to you. His good quality is going to present itself any day now—you just know it.
   C. Are different and should be given an opportunity to show you who they are and what they're made of. They should not be made to pay for an ex-boyfriend's mistakes.

8. Nice guys:
   A. Finish last. Bad boys are what you like.
   B. Fit your criteria—they're the easiest ones to walk all over and will give you whatever you want.
   C. Are quite attractive if they have the right combination of confidence and sensitivity.

9. If a man doesn't meet your expectations you:
    A. Let him down gently and move on to someone who is better suited to you.
    B. Browbeat him until he does and then you toss him aside for being weak.
    C. Stay with him anyway—it's better than being alone.

10. The three most attractive qualities in a man are:
    A. A big bank account, a fast car and no heirs.
    B. A good sense of humor, ambition and honesty.
    C. A great body, a beautiful face and a winning smile.

Your Results

You clearly know a good catch from a bad one if you chose the following answers:

1. **A.** You like to indulge in guilty pleasures but never get carried away.

2. **C.** You are mature enough to enjoy a man without making him the only man in your life, just as men choose to do with women.

3. **A.** A little flattery is nice in moderation. You don't need it constantly in order to feel good about yourself.

4. **B.** You enjoy many types of men and don't try to mold them into one category, but you also don't give the wrong man exclusive rights to you.

5. **A.** You deserve more than a married man has to offer, plus karma's a bitch.

6. **B.** Casual dating means you get to see other people so you never let it get the best of you when you come face to face with it.

7. **C.** You learn from your past but don't dwell on it giving each new suitor a clean slate.

8. C. It's okay for a man to be nice to you. In fact, you expect it and appreciate it.

9. **A.** You don't believe in wasting his time or yours so you move on when you realize he isn't the one for you.

10. **B.** You have the right idea about what makes a man special.

Chapter 12

He Loves Me, He Loves Me Not

Secret #12: Love Shouldn't Hurt

No one has ever loved anyone
the way everyone wants to be loved.
—Mignon McLaughlin

Remember when you were a little girl picking petals off flowers and uttering these sweet words, "he loves me, he loves me not?" This seemed like a rational way to determine if cute little Tommy down the street really did love you. If you were anything like me, the answer was always a resounding, "Yes, he loves me." Somehow, I always managed to rig the petal-picking process to my advantage.

As adults we play the same game, but instead of flowers, we use clues to test his love. If he sends you a text message, he loves you! If he brings you candy, he loves you! If he forgets to call, he loves you not. This can go on and on, back and forth, until you drive yourself crazy.

Love is a many-splendored thing, but it's also an exasperating thing. It's hard to know what to do when those feelings of love creep up on you and take control of your normally rational brain. You wonder if you should tell him how you feel. Will he think it's too soon? Will you scare him off? What if he doesn't say it back? If you've been reading this book chapter by chapter, you realize I've already talked a little about saying "I love you." Well, now I'm going to break it down for you blow-by-blow. (It *is* a science, you know!) And if you skipped ahead to this chapter because this issue is what's foremost on your mind, then read on. I have lots of information to share with you.

TOO SOON

I love you. *Je t'aime. Te amo. Ana Behibak.* No matter how you say it, saying I love you is a wonderful thing. It's nice to follow your heart and profess your undying love to the man of your dreams. But if this declaration comes too soon, say, before he says it first, or it's said too often (more than three times a day), or you say it when you're intoxicated (I-*hiccup*-love-*hiccup*-you-man), then your lovely message is going to send the wrong message.

The "L" word isn't going anywhere, so relax and leave it alone for a minute—or a year. Think before you speak. I know, I know, the sex is great, he's super-romantic, and he gets you. That's fabulous, but that doesn't mean an "I love you" is in order. Tell him "I want you" or "I'm crazy about you." These words are flattering and won't freak him out. The simple truth is, the giddiness you feel in the beginning of a relationship makes you think, feel, and want to say, "I love you," but what you really should be thinking, feeling and saying is, "I love how you make me feel." That's the flirtatious truth, isn't it?

TOO OFTEN

When does saying I love you lose its pizzazz? When it's said too often. You: "I love you, I love you, I love you!" Him: "Yeah, I know. You keep telling me." If this is you, maybe it's time to be a bit stingier with your romantic declarations. Save them for a special moment, when he least expects it. That's when it'll have the most impact.

Once the cat's out of the bag, when should "I love you" be said? Every time you get off the phone? No, that's too expected. Every time you have sex? Not necessarily. He'd rather hear something naughty. How about when he says it to you? Nope, even then it doesn't require an "I love you" back. You should say it when you really mean it, and no more than three times a day. Even that's a bit much.

TOO INTOXICATED

This is a big no-no, ladies. Slurring the words I love you just isn't right, especially if you've never said it before. You can say, "I like you" in a drunken gaze all you want, but you can't say "I love you." And if you do say "I sluv yous," deny, deny, deny.

Dear Tabitha,
He likes you, but he doesn't love you. He's probably seeing other women in multiple cities and fits you in from time to time. You're having so much fun because the pressures that come with a relationship are not there, and that's how he likes it.

I don't see him changing his ways anytime soon. If he wanted to spend more time with you, he would. Enjoy things the way they are—casual—or move on to something more fulfilling. Just don't expect more from your current situation.

Jula Jane

Blame it on the booze. Be very careful when giving and receiving the coveted "I love you." Make sure you mean it before you say it and, for goodness sake, make sure he means it before you believe it. He just might be drunk, too.

ACTIONS SPEAK LOUDER THAN WORDS

You may not hear the words I love you, but you'll definitely see the words in his actions. A man will go out of his way for the woman he loves. He'll move mountains and fight wars or in your case, leave work early to take you to dinner. He'll show you how he feels long before he'll tell you. Anyone can say, "I love you" and not mean it. But showing love is hard to fake. Watch his actions and do what we women do best—analyze the hell out of them.

Have you ever wondered what it means when a man sends you roses? It means you're on his mind and he's digging you. But does it mean he loves you? It's in the color of the petals. Red signifies love (yes!) while pink expresses gratitude and appreciation (thanks for the BJ). Purple says love at first sight and enchantment (I'll take it), and orange screams desire (who can blame him?). If red roses show up on your doorstep, he either loves you, or doesn't know the difference. I prefer to think it means, "I love you!"

THE LOVE DRUG

Love is the best drug on the market. It doesn't fry your brain or rot your teeth. It won't cause cancer. You can't get a D.U.I. from it. And best of all, it's free. The love drug is fairly easy to get. You just have to meet a man and breathe him in. Once you start to fall for him, the effects of the drug kick in.

Falling in love produces certain chemical reactions in the body that create an emotional high unmatched by all others. It's this high you seek so desperately. Fall in love, get high—he loves me. Fall out of love and get sober—he loves me not. When the euphoric high wears off, you end the relationship and look for your next fix—in a new mate. This seemingly innocent drug called love can be dangerous when it turns into an obsession. It's okay to be a recreational user, just don't let it get out of hand. If you find yourself going from one affair to the next, you just might be addicted to love.

BLINDED BY LOVE

Women are often blinded by love. This means a woman's perception of a man is no longer rational, logical, or even reasonable when she's in love. It's distorted, blurred and terribly altered. He can do no wrong in her eyes. She literally looks at him through rose-colored glasses, and this can be dangerous.

What's the harm in viewing your mate in the best possible light, you ask? In some cases, absolutely nothing. In fact, we should be our man's biggest fan, whether he's an average Joe or president of the United States—but only if he deserves it. That's where the danger lies. Giving respect and admiration to someone who doesn't deserve your love, or even a place in your life, can be detrimental to your health and well-being.

PHYSICAL ABUSE

It's amazing to me that in this enlightened age, men still hit women and women still take it. Nearly 25 percent of American women reported being

Dear Jula,
I'm unhappily married and don't intend on leaving my husband because I need the financial security I get from him. I am dating other men, though. I don't let things get too physical—some kissing and petting are all I allow. Somehow, this makes me feel less like I'm cheating and more like I'm filling a void.

My friends know what I'm up to and condemn me for it, especially when I do it in front of them. I don't love my husband and I don't think he loves me, so what's so wrong with a little harmless flirting?
Mia

Dear Mia,
There's nothing innocent about kissing, petting and flirting with another man when you're married. Come clean with your husband. Explain how you feel. Tell him what's missing, and ask him to help come up with a solution. He probably feels the same as you and will welcome a chance to work on it together. You may end up getting divorced, or you could just end up saving your marriage.
Jula Jane

raped and/or physically assaulted by a current or former spouse, cohabiting partner, or date at some time in their lifetime, according to the National Violence Against Women Survey. In 2001, intimate partner violence made up 20 percent of violent crime against women.

Personally, I have never been in a physically abusive relationship, but if I ever found myself in this predicament, I would leave him. No ifs, ands or buts about it. I would kick his butt out of my life and never look back. No second chances. No exceptions. Easy for me to say; I haven't been in those shoes.

I do know people who have, though, and most of them took their abusers back time and time again. For the life of me, I couldn't figure out why. Why would anyone subject themselves to such a horrible thing? Then it dawned on me. They must be blinded by love. That's the only thing that makes sense. "I know Jake is a good man. He just gets jealous sometimes and can't control his temper. It's my fault for making him mad. I should be more sensitive to his feelings," says blinded Betty sporting a shiner and a fat lip. "Carl doesn't mean to hit me. He gets so stressed out at work and loses control. I know things will be better once he gets his promotion," pleads Sue, sitting in a police station after her neighbor called in a domestic disturbance. "George is often misunderstood. He had a terrible childhood and as a result, he lashes out at those who love him, even me. I can't leave him, he needs me," cries Jennifer, as she's wheeled out of the emergency room with a cast on her right arm and three broken ribs.

A woman in love looks for the good in her man, making

Dear Diane,
He just might love you, but maybe he's not ready to say it. Once he says it, he knows things will change and it will mean your relationship is more serious. Give him time and give him space. And by that, I mean you should spend less time with him. Let him feel what it's like *not* to have you right by his side all the time and he'll realize he really does love you, and that he'd better say it before someone else does.
Jula Jane

excuses for his heinous behavior. That's often easier than facing reality. If an abused woman decides to take a stand, her life as she knows it will change. She will have to leave this man, a man she's grown to love and rely on. She'll be forced to start over, and this is just too much to bear for many women. They'd rather take an occasional blow to the body instead of a direct hit to the heart because, let's face it, if he loved her, he wouldn't hit her.

Physical abuse doesn't just happen in marriages, it also happens in casual dating. You should stop seeing someone at the first sign of abuse. A man doesn't have the right to put his hands on you unless you invite him to do so. That includes grabbing your wrist, slapping your face, or holding you down.

Physical contact between two people should be loving and tender, not aggressive and painful. It's up to you to not tolerate anything less than complete respect and to always remember, if he abuses you, he loves you not.

VERBAL ABUSE

Verbal abuse can sting just as much as physical abuse. It just stings in a different place—your heart. A lot of men try to control women with words. They believe destroying a woman's self-esteem will ensure she'll never leave. He's often right. If you beat someone down long enough, in time, they'll begin to believe what you say. A classic line used by verbally-abusive men: "You'll never find anyone better than me." He hopes that if he says it often enough, you'll believe it to be true and stay with him forever. And he's right. If you believe it, you probably won't leave. Why would you? You'll never find anyone better, so you may as well stay with him versus ending up with someone equally as bad or, God help you, worse.

"You're so stupid. You're lucky I love you, or I'd leave you for someone with a brain." This is another manipulative tactic designed to get you to stay. It's hard not to let these words affect you. They're being said by the man you love. He's attacking your self-esteem to boost his own. He loves you not. "I can't believe how fat you've gotten. Here, have another donut, Porky." If you feel insecure about the way you look, there's no way you'll look for a better man, or so he hopes. This is another form of control. His insecurity is driving him to lash out at you, the woman he claims to love. Maybe in his sick, twisted mind he really does love you, but his insecurities take center stage. He can't stand the thought of losing you, so he tries to make you believe you don't deserve better. Don't take this as flattery. It's not.

The bottom line: verbal abuse stems from insecurity. If the man you're dating is verbally abusive to you in any way, bring it to his attention and don't stand for it. "I don't appreciate the way you're speaking to me and if you continue to do so, I won't see you anymore." Give him an opportunity to change and if he doesn't, leave him. A better man is out there and he will love you, despite what you've been told.

MENTAL ABUSE

This guy is less obvious in his abuse, but equally as effective. He controls you by playing manipulative games. He understands the laws of attraction and uses them to his advantage. For example, he says, "I'll call you," but waits three days to make that call. He says, "Meet me for a drink at seven," but shows up at nine, knowing you'll wait. He says, "I love you," but flirts with other women in front of you. This kind of guy is often referred to as a bad boy and gets away with just about anything—because you let him.

His powers lie in a woman's need for the love and attention of a man, and he knows it. It's worked for years. He doesn't abuse you with words, and he doesn't come at you with his fists. He does exactly the opposite. He strokes your ego and showers you with attention—when he wants to. You become addicted to him and that's when he's got you. He knows you'll put up with anything, just to get a few more minutes of his time.

This is one of the most frustrating forms of abuse. There are no bruises and no cutting words to help you realize you're being abused, just empty promises and insensitive antics he alternates with loving remarks and sweet kisses. It's a lot easier to forgive a man for being two hours late than it is to forgive him for breaking your jaw, or is it? He loves you not.

A GLIMPSE

Your Don Juan finally calls and he finally grants you some face time, so you drop everything and go running. You arrive at precisely seven, as he asked, and since he isn't there yet, you get a table for two and wait. You order bottled water, not knowing if he'd want a bottle of wine or a cocktail. You'll wait and see. Fifteen minutes pass and still, no Don. You check your phone for a missed call. Nothing. You call your machine at home. No messages.

Another 15 minutes pass and you start to make up excuses for him. Maybe he's stuck in traffic and his cell phone went dead. The waiter returns, hoping you're ready to order something more than water. You oblige and request the baked shrimp, Don's favorite. The shrimp come, and there's still no

Don. After 30 more minutes you devour the now cold shrimp (so he won't see you started without him) and ask the waiter to get rid of the evidence.

It's now 8:00 and he's an hour late. Your mind wanders some more. Did he get stuck in a business meeting? Has he been in an accident, or worse? Is he standing me up? At this point, the waiter informs you that he can no longer hold your table. There's a party of two waiting.

You pay your bill and escape to the ladies' room, praying no one sees the stream of tears coming down your cheeks. You compose yourself and, still unwilling to give up on Don, you make your way to the bar and order a glass of wine. Hopefully, that will relieve some of the pain. It doesn't, so you try a second glass. It helps a little.

By 9:00 you're thoroughly drunk, depressed and humiliated. Your girlfriends told you he was trouble but you didn't believe them. You tried to convince them how wonderful he is. Boy, do you look foolish. You pay the bartender for the bottle of wine you ended up drinking, plus a $20 tip for listening to your tales of woe, then head towards the door. Just as you're about to step outside, Don strolls in and says, "Hey, beautiful. Sorry I'm so late. Let's get a table," and plants a delicious kiss on your sullen face. Too afraid to piss him off, you say, "No problem. I don't mind waiting for you Don," and with that you happily take his hand and walk to the hostess stand.

Mental abuse lingers because it's so much harder to recognize it for what it is. We justify it: he's busy . . . boys will be boys . . . I know he loves me . . . he's just preoccupied with work, etc. You continue to put up with it because you don't want to be without him. You even tell yourself, "It's not so bad. At least he's not hitting me." He loves you not.

SMEAR CAMPAIGN

Dear Denise,
Your problem is very common and hard to control. You have to remain calm and most importantly, never respond to him. Never answer his calls, emails, or text messages. You are to have absolutely no communication whatsoever.

The minute you respond, he'll think he has an opening. It may take some time, but eventually he will stop bothering you. If, by chance he doesn't, then you have every right to pursue legal action. This is a long and frustrating process, but an option nevertheless. Be strong.

Jula Jane

Let's say he loved you once, but now, he loves you not. Look out if he's mad and wants to get even. When you break a man's heart, you run the risk of having him lash out at you. I once read that a woman is in danger the most when she breaks up with a man.

He may not attack you physically. Instead, he could opt for the more modern approach—an online smear campaign. Brace yourself. This one hurts just as much as the others. Remember all those romantic nights of confiding in one another? You'd reveal an intimate detail about yourself or a guarded secret, and he'd share some of his. It made you feel close to him, so you divulged a little more. It seemed so innocent and tender. You trusted him and wanted to share every little detail about yourself.

Now, fast forward to the break-up. Mr. Wonderful turned out to be Mr. Wrong, so you ended it. No harm, no foul, in your eyes. He sees it a bit differently. You stomped on his fragile ego and now he wants you to feel as much pain as he does, so he launches an online smear campaign.

He can do this anonymously, so there's no real consequence for him. Here's how it goes: First he sets up an e-mail account with one of the major providers. He creates a fictitious profile and user name, and off he goes. The account is free so there won't be a name on a credit card to trace back to him.

Mr. Anonymous will spend his lonely nights and weekends posting all of your secrets and all of your intimate details online. He'll choose sites that get a lot of hits, so his slams will show up first when someone Googles your name. When he runs out of damaging information, he'll make stuff up. And I assure you, it won't be pretty. This will go on for as long as he gets pleasure from it—perhaps a week, perhaps a month, but quite possibly a year. Or until he falls in love again.

His campaign could even damage your career, if a potential employer reads about false charges of drug possession and D.U.I.s. And there's very little you can do to undo the damage. Even if you post information online contesting your ex's claims, your reputation is tainted, if not completely ruined.

The lesson here is to limit how much you reveal about yourself. Don't tell a casual date, or even an intimate partner, something you wouldn't want to see on the web. He might just spill your secrets. Great, he loves me not!

NOBODY WANTS TO BE ALONE

Physical, verbal and mental abuse play a big role in far too many relationships, often because women tolerate it. It's understandable to want someone to spend time with, to have him hold your hand and comfort you when you're just dealing with life, but it doesn't necessarily have to be a romantic partner. A good girlfriend may be just what you need. She'll grocery shop with you without complaining, watch TV with you without hogging the remote, and hold your hand, without expecting sex in return.

If you do find yourself in an abusive relationship, the best way out is through the support of friends and family. Cherish your friendships and your family as much as you cherish a man, and in your time of need, they'll be there for you. Turn your back on them, and they'll probably still be there for you. That's what friends are for. They love you, even when he loves you not.

Chapter Quiz

Are You a Slave to Love?

1. The best time to say I love you is:
   A. After you've gotten to know a man well enough to truly feel unconditional love for him.
   B. When someone says it to you—whether you share those same feelings or not.
   C. Right after a one-night stand. That way he'll know how special he is to you.

2. When a man says he loves you very early in the relationship you:
   A. Discount it as a line or figure it's his libido talking.
   B. Swoon and start to plan your wedding.
   C. Feel flattered, but you don't take it to heart until his actions prove it to you.

3. The chemical high you get from falling in love:
   A. Is the best feeling ever so you seek it at any and all costs.
   B. Is something that you are aware of so you keep its effects under control.
   C. Scares you because you are a recovering love addict and can't trust yourself to think clearly when you're in love.

4. If a man hits you or even gives the impression that he's capable of violence you:
   A. Quit seeing him for good and file a restraining order if you think it necessary.
   B. Deal with it because you love him so much and feel that eventually you can get him to stop.
   C. Hit him back and keep hitting until he stops.

5. Verbal abuse:
   A. Isn't nearly as harmful as physical abuse and should be forgiven, no matter how often it occurs.
   B. Can cause a lot of damage to your heart and soul and should not be tolerated.
   C. Is merely a way of blowing off steam. He doesn't really mean what he says.

6. A man who stands you up and doesn't call when he says he will:
   A. Is not worth your time. You kick him to the curb and free yourself up for a quality man who will go out of his way to be with you.
   B. Is a challenge. You spin your wheels trying to win his affection.
   C. Deserves to have it dished right back to him—and you're only too happy to oblige.

7. When you feel close to a man you:
   A. Badger him to share everything about himself with you.
   B. Open up but keep anything extremely private to yourself.
   C. Share all of your deepest darkest secrets as a way to bond with him.

8. If a man launches a smear campaign against you, you:
   A. Fall into a depression and repeatedly beg him to stop.
   B. Launch one right back against him—but only nastier.
   C. Take all measures available to counter the attack and save your reputation and image from ruin.

9. If you ever found yourself in an abusive relationship you would:
   A. Turn to friends and family to help give you the strength to get out of it.
   B. Hide your problems from the people who care about you because you don't want to lose face with them.
   C. Complain but do nothing about it.

10. You want a man in your life:
    A. And will settle for an abusive man versus no man at all.
    B. Because you don't feel complete or secure without one.
    C. But feel you don't need one in order to be happy. He should complement you, not consume you.

Your Results

If you chose the following answers
then you are not a slave to love but are open to love:

1. **A.** You save such important sentiments for the right time so as not to give the wrong impression.

2. **C.** You are a wise woman who knows that actions most definitely speak louder than words.

3. **B.** You recognize that being in love affects your judgment, which helps keep you on the right track.

4. **A.** You are a strong woman who refuses to be victimized and does whatever it takes to keep out of harm's way.

5. **B.** You deserve kindness and respect no matter what and won't accept anything less.

6. **A.** You don't appreciate being taken for granted so you won't allow this kind of behavior in your life.

7. **B.** You are smart enough to know that what you say in confidence may later be exposed in public—so you choose your words carefully.

8. **C.** You realize how much damage a smear campaign can cause you and will do whatever it takes to curtail it.

9. **A.** You turn to your support group to help you through tough times, no matter how embarrassed you are. Your strength combined with their love will set you free.

10. **B.** You are happy and complete on your own and will welcome a Great Man into your life when the time is right.

Chapter 13

So Long, Farewell, auf Wiedersehen, Goodbye

Secret #13: Don't Break Down Just Because You Break Up

*It's better to be healthy alone
than sick with someone else.*
—Dr. Phil McGraw

Let's sing it all together, now. "So long, farewell, *auf Wiederse-hen*, goodbye. Now, take a deep breath and let him go. There are plenty of other fish in the sea. Go fish.

Dear Jula,
I'm supposed to go out with someone next week but I don't want to. He's nice and we had fun on our first date, but I'm just not attracted to him. Can I text him to tell him I can't make it, or do I have to call?
Danielle

Dear Danielle,
Ever hear of something called karma? You can't text a break-up or a break-off. You must call. If you get his voice-mail, go ahead and break the news gently and hope he doesn't call back. Don't make up an excuse. Be honest. "I had a great time last week, but I don't feel the sparks." That frees him up to move on. Excuses from you, like "I can't make it tonight" and "I have to wash my hair," keep him holding on.
Jula Jane

BREAKING UP, GETTING DUMPED, CALLING IT QUITS

"I think we should see other people . . . It's not you, it's me . . . This isn't working." No matter how you say it, it hurts. It hurts to say it and it damn sure hurts to hear it, but it has to be said. And when I say "said," I mean *said*—certainly not texted or e-mailed.

I heard a story once about a high school girl whose boyfriend broke up with her via e-mail. He then sent an e-mail to all of their friends spreading the good news. She went to school the next day and when everyone kept telling her how sorry they were, she had no idea what they were talking about. She hadn't bothered to check her e-mail that morning, so she had no idea she'd been dumped. Ouch.

We've all been on the receiving end of a tear-jerking, heart-breaking, soul-shattering, my-life-is-over goodbye. And we've all delivered a gut-wrenching, ego-blowing, life-altering, farewell, which makes us experts in the field, right? Maybe. It depends on whether or not you've learned from your experiences and use your power for good or for evil. There's a nice way of ending a relationship and a not-so-nice way. Sending a text message saying, "It's been real, it's been fun, but it hasn't been real fun. See ya," is not so nice. Inviting your soon to be ex over for a private chat at home, letting him down easily and honestly, and topping it off with a little break-up sex, is nice.

Break-up sex! Are you crazy? You're not supposed to do that. Who says so? I think it's the polite thing to do. After all, neither of you will be getting any for a while (at least not until you drunk dial one of your ex-boyfriends), so why not give him something to remember you by? Just be clear. Be upfront: "Even though we won't be seeing each other anymore, I'd really like to go at it one last time, for old time's sake." No heterosexual male would turn that down. In fact, he'll make sure it's the best sex you've ever had. Yes, please!

BREAK-UP OPENERS

Be responsible when breaking a man's heart. Your words are going to stay with him the rest of his life. Be creative. Use something other than the typical break-up openers listed below.

1. "We need to talk."

2. "I need some space."

3. "You're a great guy, but . . ."

4. "I think we would be better off as friends."

5. "You're like a brother to me."

6. "I've lied."

7. "I don't love you anymore."

HOW
TO END IT

Dear Jula,
I met a man while in a relationship with someone else. I didn't mean for it to happen, but it did and I'm crazy about him. We've been having an affair for several weeks and it's amazing. I want to leave my current boyfriend, but I don't know how to tell him. Should I tell the truth or make it about something else?
Amy

Dear Amy,
There's no need to add salt to the wound so keep the affair to yourself. Simply tell him your feelings have changed and that you want to move on. If you confess to the affair, he's going to feel betrayed and will be more hurt than if you'd just said you'd "lost that lovin' feeling."
Jula Jane

Dear Jula,
My boyfriend of three years just dumped me for another woman. I've been trying to get him back but nothing is working. He stopped taking my calls. He won't respond to my text messages, and has quit going to his favorite bar—the one place I always knew I could find him. How can I get through to him so he'll give us another chance?
Renee

Dear Renee,
Give him space. Quit calling, stop texting, and for goodness sake, never step foot in that bar again. He has to feel the pain of losing you, even if it was at his own hand. You're suffocating him and driving him further away.

Be patient. He may not come back right away. That's okay. It doesn't mean all is lost. Move on with your life and when you're ready, start dating other men. When he hears how happy you are without him, he'll think twice about his decision. By the time he comes crawling back, you'll be in love with someone else. Ah, sweet revenge.
Jula Jane

8. "Let's make this easy on both of us."

9. "Do you remember when I said everything was all right?"

10. "Do you really want to know what I do when I say I'm working late?"

THE DUMPEE

When you are the one who's dumped, take it gracefully. Don't ask, "But *why?*" As much as you deserve an answer to that question, I beg you not to ask it. Instead, smile, kiss him on the cheek, and say, "I'll miss you baby," then walk away. Don't look back, just keep walking. Who has the power ball now? You do, Miss Thang, so keep it.

Honestly, you know why he's breaking up with you, so spare yourself the embarrassment of having him spell it out, which is exactly what he's expecting you to do. Surprise him with your response and keep him guessing. He'll never forget it.

THE DUMPER

On the flip side, when you kick a guy to the curb, handle the process as if you're ripping off a Band-Aid. Do it fast and in one fell swoop. "I've really enjoyed our time together and I think you're a great guy, but I don't feel the butterflies. I'd like to say we can still be friends but we both know that's not going to happen. I wish you all the best." Kiss and don't make up, even if he promises you a diamond ring. It's time to go.

DIGNITY INTACT

Breaking up is hard to do, and in the angst of the moment, you're going to feel compelled to humiliate yourself by wrapping your arms around his legs and pleading for a second chance. But remember, once you've lost your dignity, you're never going to get it back. You'll be doomed to spend an eternity knowing Mr. Ex got the best of you. Follow my advice and you'll be able to hold your head high and leave the past in the past without a second thought.

CONCILIATORY LINES

If you're the dumper and he's having a hard time accepting it, use one of these conciliatory break-up lines and call it a day. Don't let yourself get coerced into hours of fruitless conversation. He may say that's what he needs, but it's only going to make things worse. Let him go, then go.

1. "I hope we can still be friends."

2. "I don't want to hurt you."

3. "I'll call you sometime."

4. "I love you very much, but let's just be friends for now."

TRAPPED

Dear Jula,
I live with my boy-friend and want to break it off. There's just one problem; I don't have any-where else to go. I can't afford to live on my own, which is why I stay in the relation-ship. I know this isn't fair to me or to him. What should I do?
Rebecca

Dear Rebecca,
Your circumstances are challenging, but there *is* a way out. Look for a higher paying job then look for a roommate or two and make the move. It may be hard at first, but you'll adjust.
Jula Jane

5. "I'm just not ready to date anyone right now. I still really, really like you."

6. "You're so sweet. Thanks for understanding."

7. "You're my best friend and I love you, but you need to be independent of me right now."

8. "It's nobody's fault."

9. "I'm not putting the brakes on this; I'm just orienting it towards another direction."

10. "I'm not pushing you away. I'm not making any major decisions right now, but I'm confused, and I'm hurting, and I'm not over my last relationship."

FRIENDLY THERAPY

One friend to another: "Brad dumped you because he's in love with someone else. I'm not trying to be mean, I'm just being honest." Nobody wants to hear this. Try not to be so honest when your best friend is crying her eyes out. Console her and keep your opinions to yourself. When she's stronger, there will be plenty of time to let her know your true thoughts. She needs you now more than ever.

Friend: "There, there, now. Dry your eyes."

You: "I can't, I'm lost without him. I love him!"

Friend: "That may be so, but he's gone, he doesn't love you."

You: "You don't understand. He does love me. He's just confused right now. He needs time to think."

Friend: "You may be right. Let's focus on you for a while and give him his space."

10 POST BREAK-UP DIVERSIONS FOR WOMEN

1. Retail therapy

2. Writing in a journal

3. Cleaning

4. Watching *Sex and the City* re-runs

5. Commiserating with friends

6. Getting drunk

7. Dating someone new

8. Taking a vacation

9. Hooking up with an ex

10. Taking up a hobby

I know you know that's BS. He's not confused and he doesn't need time to think. What is there to think about? That's just a coward's way of saying, "This isn't working out. I'm moving on." Be a shoulder for her to cry on. Let her do most of the talking. Letting go of someone you love is difficult, to say the least. No doubt, one day you'll be in her shoes, so be patient and empathetic. Be what you would want her to be for you—a good friend.

Invite her over for a man-bashing, *Sex & the City* marathon pig-out session. Seeing other people in similar situations somehow eases the pain, if only for a few precious moments. Cry with her, laugh with her, stuff Twinkies in your mouth with her, and then heal with her. In the end, you'll benefit from this as much as she will.

Dear Jula,
I'm not in love with my boyfriend any-more and often fan-tasize about being single. I've felt this way for quite some time, but I can't bring myself to leave him. I don't want to be alone and fear I have the grass-is-greener syndrome. Help me find the strength to move on or find a reason to stay.
Sarah

Dear Sarah,
If you no longer love this man you owe it to him to move on. You both deserve to find love and happiness and if it's no longer with each other, then it's time to get back on the market.
Talk to him. Let him know how you're feeling and make the decision together. Chances are, if you're no longer in love with him, he's probably no longer in love with you. Maybe you can part as friends so neither of you has to be alone.
Jula Jane

Whether you left him or he left you, you have to let him go completely. Hanging on to shreds of a past relationship isn't good for either person. It's confusing and damaging. This means you shouldn't respond to him if and when he tries to contact you. His voicemails must go unanswered, his text messages and desperate pleas at your door, ignored. It's for his well-being as well as for yours. If you give him even the slightest glim-mer of hope by responding to his 200th phone call, even if it's to ask him to quit calling, he'll take it as a sign that he has a chance. What you've just taught him is that he has to be persistent; 200 calls get him a response.

There's no good reason to contact an ex. If you're lonely and just want some-one to talk to, call your sister, not him. You're horny and need a little lovin'? That's what vibrators are for. You miss him as your tennis partner? Hire an instructor to play with you. You need a date to a business dinner? Your girlfriend's hot brother will do.

You're not fooling him with any of these excuses. He knows you want to see him and are dying to get back together, and he knows that you will say anything to make that happen. If you don't believe me, ask yourself what you have thought when the roles were reversed and the guy you just broke up with kept coming up with one lame ex-cuse after the other just so he could contact you.

Calling him to ask for your forgotten sweater is also a no-no. No calls, no texts, no e-mails, no nothing. It's over. Respect him and yourself enough to let him go. That's either what you asked for, or what he wanted, so that's what it's going to have to be. Delete his phone number from all of your phones—the cell phone, home phone, work phone, and the phones of friends and family. This will make it harder, though not impossible, unfortunately, for you to reach him. Don't get caught yammering away on his voicemail about how much you miss him. Yuck.

AIN'T TOO PROUD TO BEG? DON'T!

Unfortunately, human nature takes over and manipulates us into doing things we simply shouldn't. We want the ache in our heart and the pit in our stomach to go away, so we beg and we plead and we grovel. What we don't realize is that our actions are driving him further away, exactly the opposite of what we're trying to accomplish. Here's what *not* to do if you want your ex back. (This way you'll hold onto your dignity).

1. Tell him you love him, over and over again. He knows you do. It doesn't bear repeating, especially when he's already told you he no longer loves you or even worse, that he loves someone else.

2. Apologize for how things used to be—and promise it'll be different. It takes two to tango. You're not the only one at fault, so don't take all the blame. It makes you look desperate.

3. Argue with him about why he should give the relationship another chance. You can't convince someone to love you. They either do, or they don't. Even if you did succeed in getting him to take you back, he'd be gone again very soon.

4. Feign depression or invent problems to make him feel sorry for you. He *will* feel sorry for you, but he won't respect you and he certainly won't come back.

5. Use jealousy, money, children or unfulfilled promises as a means to get him back. This will only anger him and push him farther away.

FIVE-STEP I'M-GONNA-WASH-THAT-MAN-RIGHT-OUTTA-MY-HAIR PROGRAM

"It's better to have loved and lost than never to have loved at all." Thank you, Lord Tennyson. I concur. Loving someone is a precious gift. Part of him will stay with you forever and part of you will remain with him, no matter what. Cherish that thought and move forward.

New beginnings are exciting. Focus on all the hot guys you're going to flirt with on Girls' Night out, and try to forget the past. Now you're a stronger, less naïve woman. If you're still struggling, use my tried-and-true five-step program to help you move on:

Step 1: Pack up (or preferably, discard) all of the memorabilia from your past relationship. That includes, photos, ticket stubs, hotel keys, the napkin you saved from your first date, the lock of his hair you keep under your pillow, his T-shirt that still smells like him, and anything else that will make you nostalgic.

Step 2: Give the box of mementos to a family member or trusted friend to hold for you until you're over him. Once you no longer have feelings for him—and I mean none what-soever—then and only then can you have the stuff back. I think it's nice to look back on our past from time to time, to re-flect on the good times. But only if you're in a stable enough place emotionally to do so.

Step 3: Get a makeover. I say this all the time, but for good reason. A new hair-do, manicured nails, and a new outfit make you feel good. They just do. So treat yourself. Plus, think about the look on his face when you run into him and you look marvelous. He'll be sorry he let you go.

Step 4: Get out of the house. Go to gallery openings, wine tastings, ball games, etc., and meet new people. It's time to make new friends and meet new men. Your new friends will be compelled to set you up with every single guy they know. Let them. Date, date, date until you find just the right guy. Remember, it's not just the destination, but the journey, too. Have fun along the way to finding your Great Man.

Step 5: Get a project. Dive into something new and exciting. Choose something that you've always wanted to do but never had time for: cooking classes, volunteer work, dance lessons, etc. This will take your mind off him and direct your attention onto something productive and fun. Who knows, you just might meet someone new. Anything's possible.

EASING THE PAIN

Love is cyclical. It has an oh-so-sweet beginning, a comfortable middle, and an inevitably sad end. You know this going in, so why are you so heart-broken when it finally does end? I think it's because we enter into new relationships with rose-colored glasses thinking he's the one. We imagine we'll get married and live happily ever after. And when our dreams are shattered by yet another break-up, we feel all is lost and dread having to start over yet again.

The best way to taper the pain is to welcome it with open arms. Embrace a break-up as a stepping stone to your Great Man. After all, the princess had to kiss a lot of frogs before she met her prince, and so do you. Picture your ex's face. Now, picture his face on a frog's body. Did you smile? Good.

Chapter Quiz

Is It Better to Have Loved and Lost or Never to Have Loved at All?

1. A breakup:
    A. Is an opportunity to rediscover yourself, a time to renew lost friendships and a time to reflect and come up with new plans.
    B. Doesn't bring you down you because you have a hottie on the side.
    C. Is utterly devastating and causes you to self-destruct.

2. When you no longer wish to date someone you:
    A. Quit taking his calls and hope he gets the message.
    B. Tell him in person, as gently and directly as you can—and stand by your decision.
    C. Send a quick text telling him you think you should just be friends.

3. The first person you call when you've had your heart broken is:
    A. Your ex-boyfriend. Ex sex always quells your current heartache.
    B. A hit man. If you can't have him—no one can.
    C. Your best girlfriend. She knows just what to say and what to do to make you feel better.

4. Communicating with your ex within the first three months after you break up:
    A. Is the only way to cope with your feelings of pain and loss. Hearing his voice comforts you. Even if he's rejecting you, at least he's talking to you.
    B. Is a no-no. You need to wait until you no longer have any feelings for him—love or hate. Then and only then will you be able to communicate with him without it negatively affecting you.
    C. Allows you to tell him off while you still have pent up rage fueling your fire.

5. An ex won't leave you alone. You:
    A. Tell him one last time to cease all communication with you and if he doesn't, you take legal action to make him stop.
    B. Are flattered and give him just enough encouragement to keep his pursuit alive.
    C. Kick him in the groin and yell "fire," hoping someone will come to your rescue.

6. Sleeping with an ex:
    A. Makes you feel loved and comforted, even if he has a new girl-friend.
    B. Is not a good idea unless you both are on the same page—you both agree you're "friends with benefits" or have actually rekindled your romance.
    C. Is your way of trying to win him back.

7. Getting dumped:
    A. Hurts. No matter how you look at it, it hurts.
    B. Is justifiable cause for homicide.
    C. Means you're not attractive or loveable—you're old news.

8. In order to avoid hurting a man's feelings by breaking up with him you:
    A. Stay with him but cheat on him behind his back.
    B. Act like a psycho to cause him to break up with you.
    C. Face the fact that there is no way to dump someone without causing some hurt feelings so you do it as gently as possible.

9. Remaining friends with an ex:
    A. Is better than not having him in your life at all—even if you still want so much more.
    B. Allows you to sabotage his future relationships and drive him back into your loving arms.
    C. Is possible, if neither one has any remaining intimate feelings to-ward the other.

10. The main thing to take from a breakup is:
   A. A collection of happy memories and invaluable lessons.
   B. A lock of his hair and his favorite t-shirt.
   C. His social security number and mother's maiden name. It'll come in handy for your impending revenge.

If you chose the following answers,
then you believe love is worth the risk.

1. **A.** You don't crumble, you cope, thinking, "this, too, shall pass."

2. **B.** You treat people as you yourself wish to be treated, especially when ending a relationship.

3. **C.** You face your problems with a little help from a friend.

4. **B.** You wait until you're strong enough to speak to your ex without breaking down, which makes you appear more attractive than crying on his shoulder.

5. **A.** Never one to leave things to chance, you take action before things go too far. Your safety is your prime concern.

6. **B.** You're upfront with your expectations to ensure no one gets hurt.

7. **A.** You allow yourself to feel the pain of a breakup and heal faster as a result.

8. **C.** Breaking up is hard to do, but staying together for the wrong reasons is even harder—so you don't.

9. **C.** You are realistic when it comes to friendships with exes and welcome them if and only if they are mutual and healthy.

10. **A.** You don't regret—you live, love and learn.

Chapter 14

Cheat Sheet

Secret #14: It Takes Practice to Date Successfully

If you can't get rid of the skeleton in your closet,
you'd better teach it to dance.
—George Bernard Shaw

"I'm single." "I'm divorced." "Table for one." "No, I'm not seeing anyone right now." Now, say those lines with your head held high and a smile on your face. See the difference? Being single isn't sad, it's glorious. Embrace your fabulous single self and have some fun, scratch that—make sure you have the time of your life. There's nothing standing in your way, so be whoever you want, whenever you want, however you want—and make no apologies.

Just to make sure that your efforts are as fruitful as possible, here's a quick reference guide, or cheat sheet, to dating.

Dear Jula,
What makes a man
fall in love?

Esther

Dear Esther,
A man falls in love
with a woman who
he's physically at-
tracted to first and
foremost, but also, a
woman who makes
him feel like the king
of the world. He
wants your loyalty
and respect—and
he needs your admi-
ration. When he gen-
uinely has all of those
things, he will fall in
love with you.

Jula Jane

DATE WEIGHT

"There she goes again, droning on and on about losing weight. I get it already. I have to be thin to get a date." If that's what you think, then you haven't heard my message. I don't want you to be thin, I want you to be fit and happy in your own skin. I want you to be a voluptuous size 14, who loves her body and strives to be healthy, or a spectacular size 2, who is confident in her figure and isn't afraid to eat carbs.

Getting back to your date weight means getting your body where you want it to be so you feel sexy. If you feel too fat or too skinny or too flabby, you're not going to want to meet and date men, and you're not going to attract the cali-ber of man you really want.

Every woman is unique and special, whether she's an XL or an XS. Own it, love it and flaunt it.

ETIQUETTE

I want you to make studying proper etiquette part of your im-mediate future. Buy a book or two on the subject, read it and apply it. You'll learn that "Pardon me," sounds more elegant than "Excuse me." Both are correct, but one makes you look more intelligent than the other. That's the key—look for the better of two rights and by all means, eliminate all wrongs.

I'm not suggesting you need to be prim and proper and stuffy. Not at all. That's boring. You need to be elegant and graceful and appropriate. You must know which fork to use when faced with three choices, which glass is for water and which glass is for wine, and which wine—red or white. You need to know the right way to hold your knife and fork, and where and how to place them when finished. You must know your bread plate is to the left so you don't use your date's plate to your right. And you need to know what to do with your napkin when you go to the ladies' room, and when you finish your meal.

This is just table etiquette, I also want you to learn social graces and cultural protocol. Do you know if you should address royalty directly and if so, how? Do you know not to hold hands in public in many countries? Do you know when to kiss, bow or shake hands? If you don't, then it's time you learn. You're single and dating and you just might find yourself in a situation where you need to know if you should compliment the chef with a belch or by breaking of a dish. Master the art of decorum and you will go places, ritzy places.

MAKE NICE

Mean girls and chick cliques are so passé; today's woman is strong, confident and not afraid to be nice. That means she's nice to other women, she's nice to men, hell, she's nice to *everyone* and it makes her feel great.

It's important to have a support group—a set of women whom you trust, rely on and confide in. These women will be there when you get dumped, when you need a shopping buddy and when you just need someone to talk to. Don't gossip about a friend and then make "nice" to her face. Don't tell her secrets to other people and don't throw her under the bus. Be the friend to her you want and need her to be to you.

Dear Jula,
I'm dating a guy I really click with, but there's one major problem—he's a terrible kisser. His tongue is everywhere but where it needs to be—in his own mouth. How can I teach him how to kiss me less like a frog and more like a prince without hurting his feelings?

Nellie

Dear Nellie,
A man's ego is extremely delicate, so tread carefully. Try subtle tactics, such as lightly kissing his lips and telling him how much it turns you on to feel his lips against yours. He'll take this statement and run with it in hopes of keeping you perpetually turned on. Once this sinks in, go one step further. Kiss him with a slightly open mouth and just a hint of tongue. Let him know it drives you wild when he teases your tongue with light contact. Before long, you're going to enjoy kissing this man as much as you enjoy everything else about him.

Jula Jane

Be nice to men, too. If a guy approaches you and you just aren't interested, tell him so nicely. Never roll your eyes at him or shoot him down with harsh words and please, whatever you do, don't make fun of him with your girlfriends when he walks away. People around you will see how you're treating him and will be turned off by you. Plus, you'll hurt his feelings and make him gun shy when it comes to approaching women. Don't do that to him. His only crime was finding you attractive. Be nice. Nice girls finish first!

A PAIR AND A SPARE

I'm not talking about poker and I'm certainly not talking about bowling. I'm talking about man juggling. That's right, man juggling. Date three different men and you'll always have a date. Weekend dates, weekday dates and special occasion dates—you'll always have your plus one. Date one man and you'll find yourself waiting—waiting for the phone to ring, waiting for him to ask you out, waiting, waiting, waiting.

A single woman should date two men she really likes, and one man she sort of likes. I call that a pair and a spare. There's always going to be one guy you like more than the others, that's normal. But until you're dating that one special guy exclusively, you're going to have time to kill. When loneliness kicks in, answer number two's calls, and when he's not around, answer your spare's call.

If you happen to like all three equally, then juggle, juggle, juggle. That will limit you to no more than two dates a week with each guy, which is perfect for keeping him interested but not suffocating. Dating a pair and a spare will keep your phone ringing and your dance card full, but be careful—if you get caught, you risk losing them all.

MANSCAPING

A man wants to get in your home almost as much as he wants to get in your pants. He thinks an invitation into your home is an invitation into your pants, which it often is. "Do you want to come up for a nightcap?" That doesn't mean let's drink hot chocolate and put puzzles together; it means let's drink wine and get naked.

Before you let a man see the inside of your cave, you need to do a little manscaping. Bag up your stuffed animals, even your favorite childhood teddy bear, and put them away. If you must keep one, hide it under the bed or in a drawer. You're a grown woman. Try not to forget it.

Organize your closet. He may not care if your pants are hung and your shoes, aligned, but I do. You will get ready for a date much faster if you're dressing in a tidy closet with all of your frocks and bags displayed neatly. Place dirty clothes in a hamper and wet towels in the wash. Never leave panties sunny side up in the bathroom. He may need to use it and won't you be embarrassed?

Go grocery shopping every week. Throw out old fruits and vegetables and replace them with fresh ones. Toss out leftover pizza and half-eaten yogurt—it's gross. Stock your fridge with plenty of bottled water, six bottles of beer, one bottle

COLD DIVERSIONS

Dear Jula,
How do you feel about keeping dates when you have a cold?
Hillary

Dear Hillary,
The polite thing to do when you have a cold is to call your date and explain that you have a cold, and though you'd love to see him, you understand if he'd prefer to reschedule. Most men will want you to keep the date despite your cold—and will think you a class act for giving them the option.
Jula Jane

Dear Jula,
I'm always reluctant to eat garlic or onions when on a date for fear of bad breath, but frankly, this is putting a damper on my ever exploring palette. Is there a way to indulge in my favorite eats without knocking my date over with Eau de Funk?

Trisha

Dear Trisha,
I absolutely adore garlic and indulge even when on a date—and you can, too. Bring a toothbrush with you and excuse yourself for a quick brush-up after your meal. I do this whether I've eaten odiferous foods or not—it just makes me feel refreshed and kissable. If your fabulous purse is too small to fit a toothbrush, do the next best thing—chew on a sprig of parsley followed by a breath mint. This will work wonders.

Jula Jane

each of white wine and champagne, and a six-pack of ginger ale (good for hangovers). You want him to be impressed when he peaks in your fridge (and he will peak). When he sees all that great food, he'll think you must know how to cook. The way to a man's heart is through his stomach. And being able to offer him a beer or a glass of wine will put him at ease and keep him there longer (if that's your goal).

Tidy up your living room. Fluff the pillows, dust the furniture and for God's sake, empty the ashtray, especially if you're a closet smoker. If you like to display magazines, include something for him like *Men's Health* so he'll have something to occupy him while you "make yourself more comfortable." If you read *Playboy* or *Penthouse Forum,* that's great. Just don't leave them lying around. You're still playing innocent so don't "out" yourself.

When it comes to your bathroom, I leave little margin for error. I want it clean (scrubbed every week), I want it free of debris (flat irons and makeup in the cabinet, not on the counter) and I want it gender friendly (all feminine products hidden and no lingerie soaking in the sink). Keep the mystery alive, don't show him the back story—not now and preferably not ever. Light a soft candle with a hint of jasmine.

Program your iPod with three playlists: first base, second base, and grand slam. Keep one docking station in your living room and one in your bedroom, and let the iTunes set the pace. Keep DVDs handy and leave one in the player. Choose something funny, something romantic and something sexy, like 9½ *Weeks*.

Your boudoir says a lot about you so make sure you're sending the right message. Always have clean sheets on the bed, especially if your spare just spent the night, and limit the toss pillows. They really don't serve any purpose other than slowing you down when trying to get down. Do not, I repeat, do *not* leave pictures of mom and dad or ex-boyfriends anywhere near your bed. Those belong in the living room or in a drawer while entertaining a man.

You may love Paw Paw and Tinkerbell, your adorable cat and dog, but your date may not. Empty the litter box (gag), vacuum their flying fur and run a lint brush across the sofa and chairs before your date arrives. He won't be so inclined to come back if he's covered in pet hair and slobber after his first visit. And whatever you do, don't let your pets watch. It freaks a lot of guys out. Paw Paw and Tinkerbell need to have their own beds and their own space, so keep them out of the bedroom.

Pink may be your favorite color, but that doesn't mean it belongs everywhere: on the walls, on the sheets, on the towels, on the rug. A man determines whether he could live with you or not by picturing himself in your current home. Don't make it harder on him than it already is. Limit the pink, lace and floral prints to accents only, and throw in a masculine touch here and there. You'll be shacking up sooner than later. Remember: Proper manscaping makes for repeat in-home entertaining.

CONDOM PROTOCOL

Dear Jula,
Whose responsibility is it to bring a condom on a date—the man's or the woman's?

Jill

Dear Jill,
Both the man and the woman should come prepared with a condom or two— or three or four, but when it comes time to do the deed, let him be the first to pull out a condom. This will keep him from thinking you were a foregone conclusion, plus it will reveal whether he's a man who practices safe sex or not. If he didn't come prepared and you're dying to connect, then rummage through your purse to see if you happen to have one—which, of course, you know you do.

Jula Jane

Dear Jula,
I'm dating a man from another country and though he speaks English, we're still suffering from a language barrier. We both misunderstand each other's jokes and often mistake harmless banter for slights and insults. How can we get past this?

Ingrid

Dear Ingrid,
You both recognize the problem, so now work on the solution—shrinking the gap. When he says something to you that you take offense to, bring it to his attention and explain why you feel this way. Encourage him to do the same thing when you offend him. This may seem tedious, but it's absolutely necessary for this relationship to work. In time, you'll be speaking the same language.

Jula

MOW THE LAWN

We live in a world where bleaching, sunless tanning, and teeth whitening are part of everyday life. If it's dark, we want it light, if it's light, we want it dark. Lord, who can keep up? One of the more challenging grooming processes we're faced with today? To shave or not to shave, that is the question.

There's no right answer. Some men like a full bush while others prefer a landing strip. Then there are the men who expect you to be as clean as a whistle via Brazilian waxing. *Ouch*! What's a girl with a pair and a spare to do? Go with the landing strip; it's a happy medium.

SAFETY FIRST

Dating can be deadly. Talking to strangers, riding in cars with boys, meeting online lovers and hooking up in unfamiliar places all spell disaster, unless you take pre-cautions and use your head. Here are some basic guidelines to follow when single and dating:

➤ Never give your home address or home phone number to someone you just met. Give him your cell phone number, instead. It's harder to track down your private information that way.

➤ Do not disclose your job location to a man in a bar. You may tell him what line of work you're in, as in, "I'm a waitress," but don't tell him where. If you decide not to date him and he turns out to be a stalker, he'll show up at your work.

➤ When going on a blind date, meet him at a restaurant where you know the staff. If things go bad, you have people to turn to for help.

➤ Always tell a close friend or family member where you're going and who you're with. If you turn up missing they'll know who to talk to first—your date.

➤ Don't go home with a man you meet in a bar (grocery store, library, church, etc.). Get to know him first and then decide if you trust him enough to be alone with him.

➤ Program these numbers into speed dial on your cell phone: 911 for obvious reasons; a reputable cab company for quick getaways; and roadside assistance, in case he runs out of gas or gets a flat tire as a way of entrapping you.

➤ If your date is making you uncomfortable or being too aggressive, get away from him. You don't owe him an explanation, just go. You can always tell him why when you're in the safety of your own home.

➤ No means no. If he can't take no for an answer, use whatever means necessary to make him understand and leave. You don't owe him anything, so don't let him bully you into doing something you don't want to do.

➤ Do not instigate a fight or try to make a man jealous. He may have an uncontrollable temper and cause you harm.

➤ Only accept a drink you see the bartender pour. Don't leave your drink unattended and then pick it up again.

Take it with you or ask for a new one. It only takes a split second to spike your drink with a date rape drug, so keep your eyes and hands on it at all times.

➤ Trust your instincts, they're usually right.

A FOND FAREWELL

I hope you enjoyed the book and that you will practice what I preach. It truly does work! I'd love to hear firsthand how you're faring in the dating world, so keep in touch. I can be reached at dearjula@julajane.com. You can also check out my website, www.julajane.com.

I know you can accomplish great things in your life, if you follow the secrets I've just revealed to you. That, incidentally, is the final secret. Now you know them all.

Chapter Quiz

Are You a Woman in Control of Her Dating Destiny or a Woman Who Waits for Things to Happen?

1. In order to play the field effectively you:
   A. Work hard to maintain your ideal weight and appearance, and practice your flirting techniques on a regular basis.
   B. Watch television for pointers but never make it outside to get in the game.
   C. Minimize the competition by spiking the other women's drinks with laxatives. They'll spend the night in the ladies' room and you'll be the belle of the ball.

2. Proper grooming and hygiene is:
   A. A waste of time. Men don't care about such things; they just want to get down to business, no matter what state your business is in.
   B. Necessary if you want to get attention south of the border.
   C. Something you worry about so much that it keeps you from fully enjoying sex.

3. When you see a man you'd like to meet you:
   A. Write a cute note on a napkin and send it to him through the bartender.
   B. Watch him all night but quickly turn your head when he makes eye contact.
   C. Walk right up to him and ask him to buy you a drink.

4. Practicing flirting techniques at home:
   A. Makes you feel silly so you don't do it.
   B. Makes you feel more confident when you flirt with a man in public.
   C. Is so much fun that you never leave the house. Why settle for hamburger when you have lobster at home—you.

5. If you don't have a date on a Saturday night you:
   A. Stay home and eat three containers of ice cream while watching *Never Been Kissed.*
   B. Call up every ex in your little black book with an offer of a good time.
   C. Invite a girlfriend out for dinner and cocktails. You don't need a man in order to have a good time.

6. Other women:
   A. Are competition and should not be trusted.
   B. Are potential wing-women and lifelong friends.
   C. Serve no purpose—you can't date them and you already have a core group of friends.

7. When you see a woman sitting alone at a bar you:
   A. Hope she meets someone soon because it's painful for you to see her sitting there all alone.
   B. Think she's either a hooker or a desperate woman looking to pick up a man.
   C. Don't give it much thought. Men and women sit alone at bars all the time—maybe she's relaxing after a long day or just out to enjoy a cocktail. Or maybe she's going through flirt boot camp, just like you.

8. You repay a man for an expensive meal by:
   A. Sleeping with him. That's what's expected, isn't it?
   B. Saying thank you.
   C. Gracing him with your presence.

9. Being single:
   A. Is fun, liberating and a time to live life to the fullest.
   B. Makes you feel unattractive and insecure, especially in large groups and at parties.
   C. Is not something you worry about. You always have a "next" before you have an ex.

10. Self-help books are:
   A. For desperate people with no life.
   B. Inspirational and invaluable when trying to improve your life.
   C. Warm and fuzzy substitutes for men and dating.

Your Results

**Your dating destiny is your own
if you chose the following answers:**

1. **A.** You've gotta pay to play you always say and you're willing to pay with your time and effort.

2. **B.** Your day starts with a shower and a shave because you never really know how it will end.

3. **A.** Not one to be too forward, you use subtle tactics to get your point across.

4. **B.** Practice makes perfect and you most definitely are willing to practice.

5. **C.** You enjoy your friendships and choose to spend quality time with the girls.

6. **B.** You are a secure woman who enjoys making new friends.

7. **C.** This is a new era where women should be able to enjoy dining alone in public—with or without a book in hand.

8. **B.** You are courteous and confident.

9. **A.** You're single because you choose to be and you're not about to apologize for it.

10. **B.** You are proactive and use whatever means available to improve your life.